THE RE-RELEASE OF A BEAUTIFUL STORY

A spiritual guide that will help you heal
from your past, defeat your enemies
and walk into your purpose

Na'Toria Campbell

BALBOA.
PRESS
A DIVISION OF HAY HOUSE

Balboa Press books may be ordered through booksellers or by contacting:

Balboa Press
A Division of Hay House
1663 Liberty Drive
Bloomington, IN 47403
www.balboapress.com
1 (877) 407-4847

The images on the front and back cover were photographed
by photographer, Blue Franswa.

Print information available on the last page.

ISBN: 978-1-5043-6013-5 (sc)
ISBN: 978-1-5043-6014-2 (hc)
ISBN: 978-1-5043-6054-8 (e)

Library of Congress Control Number: 2016909878

Balboa Press rev. date: 06/28/2016

Dedication

I dedicate this book to all people who are battling emotional hurts, abuse, sickness, pain or any form of dis-ease. I pray that this story guides you to discover where the source of healing begins and ends. I hope that it inspires and motivates you to live out your dreams without limitations. Ask God for everything that your heart desires, and if you honor him, he will give it to you. Have faith and know that he is with you. I encourage you to move forward and live out your wildest dreams with love and peace surrounding your heart and mind. God loves you more than you know, and I love you too.

Contents

Acknowledgements

I give all thanks and gratitude to my Lord and Savior, Jesus Christ. Without him, I would not have accomplished this task of writing this story. I give all glory and honor to the King.

To my two beautiful children, the two of you are my strength. When I was weak, God sent you to help strengthen me. I am forever grateful to have you in my life, and I love you both dearly.

I want to give special thanks to my family, friends, sorors, and church family who have supported and encouraged me throughout the years. I also want to acknowledge my editor, Nancy for your superb and professional editing services.

Lastly, I want to give thanks to Freda. Writing this story helped me to release my hurt and heal my broken heart. Thank you for being my character, my Aaron, and my voice. I look forward to us sharing more stories to help break the vicious cycle of hurt and pain in the world and restore it to peace, harmony and love.

A Letter from the Author

Dear Love,

Since the start of this amazing, yet challenging spiritual journey I have evolved tremendously as a person and a writer. Writing this story helped me to rid myself of the emotional issues that were holding me back from becoming my greater self. It was my first wobbly step from out of my comfort zone as a writer. Yes, it was scary. Whenever I felt too wobbly, God would send someone or something to help me stand up, and each time I would stand up with more balance and confidence.

When I write, I feel like I am creating a new world. A safer world. A place where I am free just to be myself. It feels like for once I have a voice that is loud, bold and courageous enough that it forces others to stop and listen. Through my writing, the introvert becomes an extrovert in BIG BOLD INK that will continue to ROAR even after I am laid to rest. Yes, I have evolved!

Although this story is about my Christian faith, I now embrace the spiritual component of all religions that teach and practice the concept of love, because that is God. To me, true love is choosing to do what is right for yourself with the knowledge that it will benefit others. So, in this aspect of love, you are not only healing yourself when you implement better choices for your life, but you are helping to improve the world.

To reach God, who is within you and all around, one must find a way to connect with God. My way of connecting with God inside of me is through Jesus, who is my Lord and Savior. Jesus came to heal me from the emotional wounds that I had been carrying around from my early childhood that was creating sickness and disease in my body. Not only did he heal me but he taught me how to heal myself naturally, day by day so that I could continuously heal.

Healing is an ongoing journey and the more you embrace it, the better life becomes. I have accepted other spiritual teachers in my life to help guide me through this journey as I recognize the Godly light within them. For me to get to this place that I am at now in my spiritual walk, I had to step away from the church building for a while so that I could let go of religion or legalism. I lessened as much of the distractions from my outer environment as I could, including limiting the amount of time spent watching television and socializing so that I could hear more clearly from God and work on changing my mindset for the better. I believe that sharing your spiritual experiences through your personal and intimate encounters with God is what heals the underlying emotional wounds and trauma. I endured childhood trauma and the decision I made as a young girl to hold on to those hurtful memories of my past stifled and suffocated me from becoming who God created me to be, which is simply Me.

The purpose of sharing this story is to help guide you through the process of change and spiritual growth so that your mind can be set free to live the life that you want. During the writing process, I had to break through "generational curses" to build up my courage to publicize this personal story. If you take out the religion aspect, this means changing the thoughts in your subconscious mind that were passed down from your ancestors and environment that creates fear and other negative thoughts that hinder you from reaching your greatest potential.

Fear, to me, is the opposite of love. It can cause you to do some dangerous things to yourself and others if you are not careful with it or if you are unaware you are operating in it. If you want to see a modern-day miracle performed so that you can let go of past hurts and disappointments, accept the truth about your current reality, make a decision to switch your mindset to the affirmative realm, and act accordingly. From my experience, change is not an easy feat, especially when you are accustomed to operating a certain way. However, you should never give up or doubt yourself; just try a different approach and measure its effectiveness by monitoring your actions, mood and energy level.

Become aware of the thoughts that have kept you in bondage and choose to change them, which can also involve letting go close friendships or close ties that you have with loved ones. It does not mean that you do not care or have compassion for them anymore, but it does mean that you recognize that you had to let go of the close encounters to embrace a new and different way of life. It may mean moving away from home or a city you have grown accustomed to living to establish new friendships and companionship with those that are living the change that you are making or have made, or it may mean accepting someone in your life that has always been there, but negativity blocked the relationship from forming. It could also mean letting go of a bad habit or addiction in exchange for a healthy and stable lifestyle. The change for the better is deciding to love yourself by doing what is right for YOU with the knowledge that all those connected to you will also grow and heal because of the positive changes occurring in your inner and outer world. Love is God, and he lives inside every one of us. Loving yourself will shine his loving Godly character outwardly in the world, and that my friend is love.

I pray that as you read this personal story of a young woman named Freda who was my first client; will open up your mind so that you can let go of the negative thoughts and perceptions. Freda, who is also affectionately called Free, is a fictitious name. The names of the other parties in the story were changed for privacy reasons. I can empathize with Freda's story. Her story is my story as she is a mirror image of myself. When I look in the mirror, I not only see Freda, but I can feel her hurt, shame, and disappointments. I can feel the sickness and pain that she experienced living with a chronic illness. I felt the anxiety, worry, and fears that she faced when she had to raise two children as a single parent while learning how to live with a chronic illness.

I can also feel her triumphs and success as she renews her strength and power after being knocked down by the harsh realities of life through her faith and the love of Jesus Christ. I can put myself in her shoes because I am Freda and Freda is me. I had to "Free" the hurt little girl inside of me. Freda was created to help me to overcome my writing insecurities so that I could release this book again and free myself of the hurt that was inside of me.

Yes, this is the second edition of the first book I wrote, "A Beautiful Story." After releasing the first version of my story, I still struggled emotionally in my relationships even after reconnecting with my dad. Freda helped me to revisit my past so that I could get off of the cycle of hurt and move forward in my journey. There is a quote I heard that radiates in me as true, "before you can help someone else you must first help yourself." Therefore, I had to help myself before I could effectively help those that I am assigned to help let go of their hurt and reach their true calling.

Through this journey, I have come to see reflections of myself in others whom I am connected. It helps bring forth understanding so that I can operate with compassion and less in hate or fear. I pray that as you read this story, you begin to see through your internal darkness and break the chains that have held you captive so that your heart and mind is free to live in peace, love and harmony.

With love,

Na'Toria

Freda's Introduction

I always felt like I had something tremendously important to say, but whenever I tried to speak, my words would go to left field when everyone I needed to share them with were in right field. Whenever I would find the courage to say what was in my heart, I felt like my communication skills were inadequate or not clear enough because the person I would be speaking to seemed as if they did not fully understand me.

After several failed attempts at trying to get the person to know me, I would quietly retreat inwardly and shy away from the conversation. It was as if I had someone in my head saying, "If you say it, then they will think that you are crazy, so you better not say anything or else…" My voice became inaudible almost to a whisper. People often told me to speak up, or they would yell, "I cannot hear you," whenever I became courageous enough to share some form of information in front of people. The attacks became, even more, blatant when I received assignments back from my teachers with red ink scribbled all over them that blared, "Not good enough," or "Unacceptable." The criticism would speak to my spirit and say to me, "Your grammar skills are weak. You wrote 'is' when you should have written 'are.'" Constant criticism shattered my voice, dreams, and desires. Did I just perceive it that way because I internalized it negatively instead of constructively? Either way, I allowed it to place fear and doubt inside of me. I limited myself from becoming and revealing my real self because I held on to the attacks from the evil spirits or negativity that I chose to accept. I allowed them to rest inside of me to torture and taint my mind, body, and soul.

Most of my life I did not talk much about the events that occurred in my early childhood or about the things that I knew deep down that I should be saying because I felt shunned. I did what felt safe to me, so I crawled into my quiet corner, sat down, drew my legs in near my heart, wrapped my arms around them and wept. I stayed in this position for most of my life until I found my voice.

Chapter One

The Challenge: Answering the call that leads to discovering your purpose

"For many are invited, but few are chosen." --Matthew 22:14

The challenge that I faced when answering the call of God was that I felt as if I could not verbalize my thoughts in a way that would deliver a clear and crisp understanding to people. I would have the most formalized messages or words that would come to me from somewhere deep within. I had this strong desire to share it with others. However, when I would build up enough courage to say what was in my heart and mind, the words just fumbled out of my mouth or onto a piece of paper like a wide receiver fumbles a ball, and I lost the message. It was as though my thoughts and feelings could not travel down my vocal chords and out of my mouth. I could not even scribble them on a sheet of paper in enough time to share them. Whew! Thank you, God, for computer programs like Microsoft

1

Word, because now I can type just as fast as I can think it. What I had to say was not from me but him—from the one God sent to save us; you know his name: Jesus.

I struggled with sharing the messages or words that were in my heart with others because of not only the constant criticism that highlighted my inadequate speaking and writing skills but also because the internal battles blocked me from sharing the Good News. How could I help and teach others how to live when I was grappling with my salvation? I was trying to understand the unfolding mysteries God was revealing to me all while sinking into the bottomless pit called Hades. I kept the words in my head and heart. Then I took the words and myself back to God.

I endured some major childhood trauma. God was the only one I felt safe revealing my true self. I often retreated to that place within me where I knew God existed, and I stayed there for nearly thirty-two years until I stepped out in faith and discovered my voice.

Before then, I was living aimlessly. I was so frustrated with the world, people, and myself for not living life the way I knew God instructs his children to live, and I would just shut down. I would try not to speak at all, or when I would decide to converse with others, I would talk about fundamental issues or generic concerns and topics.

Now, I understand what my purpose in life is, and I see why those offensive linemen were in a position to block me—the receiver and deliverer of the Good News. I allowed certain situations to knock me down. It often left me feeling as if I was beaten down, mocked, and scorned. I received blow after blow to shut me up and shut me down, but you know what? The more blows I took, the stronger I felt and the harder I fought back.

I am finally delivering the Word of God to you, so that goes to show you who won. All of the red ink, the mockery and the "you are not good enough" thoughts or comments were all LIES! You see, what I am sharing will help you change your life. It will inspire and motivate you to become your greatest self, and you will begin to believe and operate in faith towards living a life of purpose.

Deep down in my soul, I kept receiving burning messages, and they were screaming at me saying, "You have something to say, and they will listen." I also had other issues that blocked me from sharing these powerful and prophetic messages that came from God. One of the problems I dealt with was feelings of inadequacy in my walk with Christ. My life at the time when he called me from the burning bush was not the epitome of an example of Jesus' life. I was backsliding down mountains of sin towards the depths of Hades. So who was I to share these powerful life-changing words during a time when I needed a life makeover?

In a sense, I felt just like Moses. You know, the man from the Bible who led the Israelites out of Egypt. Well, let me give you a snippet of the story of Moses. God called Moses one day from out of a burning bush. He told Moses that he was sending him to the Pharaoh, the king of Egypt, to request that he release God's people, the Israelites, out of captivity. God heard his children's cry for help, so he chose Moses to go and convince the Pharaoh to release them. He created Moses for this mission. However, Moses did not think that he was the best man for the job. He had a speech impediment, similar to my speech and writing issues, so he told God that he had chosen the wrong person. Moses felt that he could not speak well nor was he confident in himself to go before the leader and demand such a request. To add to Moses' dilemma, he had just murdered a man, and he was in hiding from the Pharaoh.

Now, imagine yourself in Moses' shoes. What would you have said to God? How would you have felt receiving such a request from the Creator? God asked him to go back to a place where he killed someone and become a leader. The task seemed incomprehensible, yet God said to Moses, "Yes, you can do it, and you will lead my people out of slavery." He gave Moses all of the instructions and tools that he needed to lead the Israelites out of bondage. God also advised Moses to have his brother, Aaron, speak for him. Aaron's purpose was to help Moses build up his confidence, and that is how he overcame his insecurities. Yes, Moses accomplished the monumental task of delivering God's children from out of the pharaoh's stronghold just as God instructed him to do. That was Moses' purpose. It was the reason God created him, which is why his legacy lives today.

Think of how Moses' life may have turned out had he not followed God's plan. The offer was honorable but carrying out such a request seemed unrealistic because of the life Moses was living at the time. Even still, Moses chose to step out in faith and accept God's command for his life. He carried out God's mission with fidelity. Like Moses and Aaron, God has a divine plan for my life, and he has one for you as well.

Oprah Winfrey said a quote that radiates in my being as truth. "Your real job in life is finding out your purpose." I made it my goal to find out exactly what God's plans were for me to fulfill because I was tired of resisting the burning passion and desires of my heart. The Bible says that before you were born, God had a plan and purpose for your life. Yes, we are all here together for a divine purpose. Jeremiah 1:5 says, "Before you were in the womb I knew you; before you were born I set you apart."

God has a way of giving me signs to let me know whether I am on the right path or not. From as far back as I can remember, I always felt connected to another source, a higher source. I had a sense of safety and protection that came from some secret place. Even when I felt the worst and faced monumental challenges, I still believed that I would overcome them. In my heart, I felt as if I would get through the problem and become better than I was before it occurred. The words that God sent to me are not just for me, but they are for you as well.

In 2009, I received an urging message to share my life in written form. The problem I had with that calling was that I did not and still do not consider myself a great communicator. Although I had earned a master's degree by that time, I did not feel my writing skills were at the level needed to produce writing that was good enough to share with the world. As I struggled with the notion of not being good enough, something inside of me said, "Get it out, Freda. Get it out now."

Then I began to choke because I did not want to expose my hurts, disappointments, and shame to the world. To be honest, I did not want people seeing my vulnerabilities, especially those persons who had caused so much hurt in my life. I did not want to lead my enemies into my private life. In my mind, I thought that the less they knew about me, the less damage they could do to me. I tried my hardest to keep the very thing that God wanted me healed and delivered from hidden because I did not want to face others as well as myself.

To make things plainer, I did not want to become exposed. I did not want others to know just how badly my internal injuries were affecting me. I also did not wish to look at myself and face my demons because I knew it would hurt too badly. However, I could not keep it inside of me any longer because I was running out of bandages. It was becoming harder and harder to cover the internal injuries from my past because they were oozing over into my present.

I was also dealing with thoughts of what the people near and dear to me would think, like my family and friends. You see, I am an extremely private person, and I absolutely did not want my hurts, thoughts, and dreams exposed to the world.

Initially after hearing the call to share my life story, I decided not to answer it because of fear. My fear was comparable to the role of those big offensive linemen because it kept tackling me to keep me from catching the ball. I felt like no one was going to be able to receive what came from me anyways, so I dropped it. Who was I? Really, who was I to share my story about how I found God when my life did not exemplify living a Christ-like life at all? At the time, I was inconsistently visiting the church I had joined. I was not serving in ministry. To be honest, I have never served in my church.

I was what you would call a spectator or watcher. I was watching others in the church do all the work, while I sat back, relaxed and listened to the preacher. Then I would be quick to call out someone else's flaws while neglecting to see my shady behaviors. I was very similar to how a fan acts at a game. I sat down, stood up and cheered. Then I cried when my team won or lost. You could find me in the stands fussing and shouting at the team when they did something I did not like or understand. I did none of the hard work the players did to prepare and train for the game. I did not study my notes, or, in this case, the scriptures, and I prayed when I needed or wanted something. I did not give up anything or make daily sacrifices as a player does when he is training in the hot sun away from his family and friends for months at a time. Some of the insecurities that I faced resulted from the choices that I made. I was not ready to accept this fact because I did not want to acknowledge my faults. Not wanting to face my faults is the main reason I did not feel confident in my abilities to answer God's call. The more I resisted him, the more I felt a choking sensation.

The reason God called me to share my personal story was simple: so that I could heal. He needed me to heal so that I could become an example to help lead others to Christ so that he can heal them, too! He has to heal you first so he can train and prepare you to operate in your divine purpose. To tell you the truth, God did not create us to live in misery or unsatisfied contentment. God called me to share my life with you because he wants me to reveal the truth so that you can stop living a lie. His truth will lead you out of bondage and improve your life so that your mind can enter into rest. Then you can build and prosper in every area of your life.

I call the words that I receive "the truth" because they come from a place beyond my understanding and source of knowledge. At the time that I received God's call, I had just begun to receive revelations of things to come. I did not have a lot of biblical knowledge. However, I had just started receiving teaching from my bishop that brought about a deeper level of understanding, connections and confirmations of things I had known all along. I had not known them because I had no biblical or spiritual background to confirm them as true until I opened up and allowed Jesus to instruct and teach me the Godly way to live. All I had was an unyielding sense of right and wrong.

I followed a decent, orderly conduct based on the world's standard. I made good citizenship in school, kept my grades high, earned a scholarship, and became an educator. I was an overall good and decent all-American girl. The only negative that popped out for the world to see was that I became pregnant and had a baby out of wedlock.

Nowadays, the world has an approval code stamped on people who decide to create children without having a helpmate. It has become common for some people to produce children out of order. It is difficult for some single parents to live a productive lifestyle when they do not have consistent physical support. However, I must say that my son, even though his conception was out of order, helped to save my life. God turned my negative situation into something positive. My son gave me hope and the drive to keep living during times when I wanted to give up and die. God is so amazingly magnificent! He did that because he had a plan for my life.

Apparently, God knew something about me that I did not and could not even comprehend about myself. He knew that I had the ability to experience trials and to triumph over them. Believe me, when I say that God will not send you more than you can bear, so whatever challenges that you are facing are set up for you to overcome them. He is placing you in the refinery, watching and waiting for the silver inside of you to form so that he can transform you into gold. Refer to 1 Corinthians 10:13 for evidence.

After a while, I began to accept my calling to share my testimony. I even began to share with my close family members and friends my desire to write a book. They all encouraged me to go for it. However, I was still very hesitant. I attempted to share my story on several occasions, but I could never complete the task. I did not want people outside of my comfortable close-knit family and friends to know about my life. The people closest to me did not even know some of the deep-rooted emotional issues that were brewing inside of me. I was selective about what I shared with them, so how could I fathom the thought of exposing my life to people who I felt did not know or care about me?

I know that I am not the only person in this world to withhold their true self from others. I used to think before I discovered my purpose, which is a lot of us would not become who we are truly meant to be in this life because we are running and hiding from our true self just as I had done for so long. Now, I know that my old way of thinking was an LIE, too.

The truth is that if you do not become who you are destined to be, then it is because you just do not believe. For instance, I was holding back my authentic self and becoming what I felt was acceptable to the world because I did not believe in God's promises for his children. I believed the lies that Satan—the enemy—told me, and by doing so, I limited myself from becoming my greater and even highest self.

My lack of belief in God's promises came from the fact that I honestly did not know any better, but now I know better so, therefore, I do better. God created me for a divine purpose, just as he has created you for a specific role to help build up his kingdom. There are many people living short lives due to lack of understanding and wisdom. The constant attacks of life are designed to keep you in need and strife. The enemy does this to keep you on the cycle of hurt, disappointments, and lack. He wants to keep you in the darkness. He wants to block your view of the light so that you remain dependent upon his system, believing in his lies.

I discovered where that source of light comes from, and I have been standing in the light praying, fasting, and healing so that I can deliver this message to you. Allow me to point some spiritual light in your direction with this scenario so that you can begin to identify how to discover the person that you are to become. As you read the situation, take notice of how the enemy sets up traps to keep you on his dark and vicious cycle.

When you experience feelings of excitement or rush from the thought of becoming someone grand and respected, shortly after reality hits. Next, doubt sets in your mind. Then your dreams begin to fade away. The euphoric feelings you had after envisioning yourself becoming someone who is happy, successful, and fulfilled stems from the desire within you that is drawing you towards your divine purpose. Traditions passed down from man, and false religious teachings have created fear in many, and that fear is what withholds your authentic self from forming—fear of the outcome and of the unknown possibilities, fear of what others will say and think. This fear then causes you to accept the status quo and live a life based on the norms of society.

For instance, a person may say that he or she wants to become a nurse or science teacher. At the heart of things, you want to become a doctor or scientist that leads a team to find the cure for an incurable disease. I am not downing nurses or science teachers. We surely need them in our life. What I am saying is that when you allow God to lead you, he will put you in a position to become not just an ordinary nurse or teacher but an extraordinary one who is operating in a divine purpose.

When you ignore or miss his great call for your life, it opens the door for apathy to walk in and fester inside of you. The spirit of apathy leads you down a spiral slope that spins you downward to self-destruct and die before you have had the chance to live. Does this sound similar to what you are experiencing or have experienced in the past? If so, continue reading, and use my life story as your guiding light.

I was living the status quo lifestyle. You know, just going to work, barely paying the bills, partying and getting drunk sometimes just to have fun. I went to church here and there so that I could get through yet another cycle of hurt or disappointment. I was only existing, passing the time away, but not living because I felt so unfulfilled with my life. It felt like something was missing in my life so I would do things to try to fill the hole. I bought several new cars that I did not need, and bought a house even though I was not ready financially, emotionally, or spiritually to make any significant financial commitments.

Living the status quo lifestyle, just existing, and not living the life that I desired, gave clearance for an awful apathetic spirit to enter my being. I battled with this emotion for a very long time, even in my teenage years. My attitude was nonchalant, but that is the spirit of apathy. I was so bland that you could not tell if I was happy, sad, hot or cold. Apathy has a way of taking the zest out of your life. I was literary a walking zombie who did not care if I lived or died. Eventually, when you operate this way, you become tired and weak. The blows of life begin to take away your tears and that cold spirit called bitterness starts to set into your bones. Yes, it happened to me just as I see it happening to so many others.

Throughout my life, God would order me to do something courageous. I would completely ignore him and do what I wanted or what someone else wanted me to do. Of course, afterward, I often found myself in some trouble that led me scrambling back to God requesting his help to deliver me from the situation. As always, he would show up and help me feel better. Then I would turn right back around and head back towards my self-destructive behaviors. I was like the children of Israel who Moses led out of slavery. After God came into their lives and showed them signs and miracles, they would immediately forget. Then they would begin complaining and making more requests to him. I became accustomed to asking for more after God would deliver me from a situation or bless me with something that I was undeserving of receiving.

My life was an emotional roller coaster ride filled with unexpected drops to dark and small places. I would allow God to come in my life, and he would twist and twirl me back on track towards that high place, over and again. I would always come close to reaching the top, the height of my potential, but then I would spiral back down to my favorite dark resting place, in a corner, curled up crying, shaking and afraid.

To further my defiance and disobedience to follow God's calling to share my story, I came up with a clever way to do it without exposing my identity. I decided to write a fictional story that gave the essence of the message I had to deliver to people. You see, I thought I could outsmart God and you by finagling my way out of doing what he had instructed me to do. I created a fascinating and captivating character to deliver the story that God wanted me to share, but then the story stopped.

Afterward, I tried many times to write the story, but I could never finish it. It took me several years before I began to realize why I could not complete it. It was because I was manipulating it in a way to make it seem as if my issues were the result of someone else's errors, hiding my true self from others. I was not holding myself accountable for my actions and decisions because I was afraid to look at myself in the mirror. I formed some very intriguing storylines that would have kept you glued to the pages. The details of what has happened in my life are so descriptive and captivating, but something stopped my flow of words from continuing. Then I stopped altogether, and I did not attempt to share my story, until the summer of 2012.

Since 2009, after my initial struggles with sharing my story about my tumultuous childhood, I have been on several high-rise and topsy-turvy roller coaster rides. One of the rides I went on was called love and marriage. You probably think that a wedding is a positive and happy experience. For me, it was not. It marked the beginning to the end of my life, as I had known it. The stress throughout the wedding planning process made the entire experience horrible for me. Childhood friends who I held close to my heart and still do to this very day were feuding and backing out of the wedding. A few of them did not speak to me for a while. Somewhere in the process, my fiancé checked out of the relationship. I was blind to my pending relationship doom because I was distracted by the whole disastrous wedding planning process. Oh, and did I mention that my work environment was like the twilight zone? That is a whole other story that I am not going to try to explain. You would have had to experience the work environment to get the full depth of what was going on at my place of employment. My colleagues who were there along with me during this time will be able to relate to what I am saying. Within that same year, I got married, pregnant and had a baby all while working in a spiritual war zone called my place of employment.

The undue stress I was carrying around caused me to have an unexpected preterm delivery at twenty-seven weeks gestation. I watched my premature baby live in an incubator with several tubes attached to her small, frail body for several months, and all that I could do was sit and wait. Watching her fight for her life was one of the most traumatic episodes that I endured in my lifetime. To watch my precious and fragile baby for two months live in an incubator with the uncertainty of whether or not she was going live and if so, if she would have health issues was torturous. However, this situation worked in my favor because I became very close with God. I prayed and wrote to him daily. One of the main ways that God communicates with me is through my writing.

Sadly, by the time the spring of 2010 arrived, I was dealing with raising two children on my own because my husband, now ex, and I had separated. Eventually, later that same year we divorced. For the sake of privacy, I will not divulge the details of the demise of the relationship. However, please notice that I was being attacked by the enemy from every angle very quickly. It seemed as if the enemy had a personal vendetta out for me. He was intentionally trying to wipe any remembrance of me from off the face of the earth. I felt like I was an emotional train wreck headed towards death.

Near the end of 2010, I began to develop health issues. I later discovered that I had developed a condition called rheumatoid arthritis, also known as RA. RA is a chronic or long-term autoimmune disease that causes inflammation and pain in your joints. The immune system attacks the healthy cells in your joints. In extreme cases, it can attack some of your organs, like your lungs and heart. It is very similar to Lupus. By the time the year 2011 arrived, I was literally in agonizing pain and shame.

Ok, so let us do a timeline: In March of 2009, I got married. Shortly after the wedding ceremony, my husband and I faced challenges. Then I battled a difficult pregnancy, which led to having my baby prematurely. Oh, and do not forget that I worked in a very toxic environment as well. In 2010, I nursed my baby girl in the neonatal critical intensive care unit for two months watching monitors, praying and fasting all while battling with the steady decline of my new marriage. Then shortly after my baby's arrival home from the hospital, I was back to being a single parent of two children versus one child, and I was divorced. Before the year ended, my health started failing.

The health struggles, raising my two children as a single parent and my grief stemming from the divorce began to consume me. All of the stress was too much for this shell of a body to hold all at once. I started to deteriorate quickly. I was in constant pain, so much at times that I could barely walk or use my hands. I felt ashamed and vulnerable about my failed marriage and declining health. My weight dropped drastically, my hair began to fall out, and my skin was breaking out in irritable itchy unattractive rashes.

Now, I know you are probably saying, "Whoa! Where was God during all of this mess?" Well, I am here to tell you that if it had not been for God being with me through it all, I would be dead today. It took something greater than you and me to put me back together and transform me into the beautiful and new person that I am today.

I pray that as you read this, you will begin to transform your thoughts and actions into the positive and optimistic realm so that you can live out God's purpose for your life. He wants you to live happily, plentifully, and in good health. Some of you reading this may already be living the life God wants you to live. Maybe my story will help you to enhance your life or bring confirmation from Heaven that God is indeed good all of the time. The sad reality is that the majority of you are not living but merely co-existing in a world of spiritual turmoil and strife, awaiting your next boomerang effect.

Now, let me rewind my story all the way back to its original beginning, my birth so that you can get a betting understanding of how my life came crashing down so quickly.

Chapter Two

The Healing Process Begins Here: Traveling back to your past

"Daughter, your faith has healed you. Go in peace." —Luke 8:48

My story truly began on November 3, 1979. I was born into the world of full of limitless opportunities and transgressions. My mother, Jeanine, went into labor at home. She called my dad (his name is Curtis, but everyone calls him, Curt) to help her. She crawled to the bathroom where he was taking a bath; she asked him to take her to the hospital. He was upset with her over something, so when he heard her cry for help, he looked at her and rolled his eyes. Then he took his precious time getting dressed. When they finally arrived at the hospital, my mother was in so much pain that she felt nauseous. In the hospital room, she called my dad's name and motioned for him to come closer to her. As he walked closer to her, she threw up all over his dapper attire. I guess that was my mom's way of retaliating.

My dad and mom named me Freda Jenay. My Uncle Lonnie and a friend of his came up with the name and my mother loved it. However, growing up, I did not like my name. I preferred to be called me by my nickname, Free. People ought to be very careful and selective when they choose a name for their child because an individual's name says a lot about them.

For instance, my name is of German origin, and it means "peaceful." It also means "beautiful beloved" in Scandinavia. The American meaning of my name is "good counselor." Ever since my birth, I have felt as if I have been on a path of discovering who I am. Looking back at my history, my choices and decisions I now recognize that I have become exactly what my name means. I am a peaceful, beautiful beloved good counselor. However, I had to fight many unpleasant thoughts disguised as ugly demons before I recognized my true identity and the purpose I am to fulfill here on earth. It was not until I decided to accept Jesus and began to follow his way of living that I began to see myself for who I am. Before that time, I was leaving life on my terms and falling deeper and deeper into the pit of Hades because of my sinful thoughts and behavior.

Today, I make decisions that will lead me closer towards success. I may not make the mark all of the time, which is why I remain humble even when I reach a milestone. Humility keeps me grounded so that I do not become too prideful and run ahead of God.

I am at a place in life where I can now impart wisdom to others. As I learn and grow, I make choices that will purposefully lead to favorable results. Although, there are times when I missed the mark as I am not perfect. I have the freedom of knowing that I do not have to walk in shame, guilt or defeat as I did in the past. If I miss a step and fall, I get back up with the wisdom that it takes to get back in line so that I can continue the journey towards victory. I hope that through my name, you begin to identify with the meaning of your name because it plays a role in defining who you are. As I learn more about myself, I realize that I like being me. For so long I despised myself. I appreciate my parents for deciding to procreate so that I could live, and I thank them for giving me the name Freda.

Ok, now let me get back to telling you about my parents. They were teenagers fresh out of high school when they married. My dad joined the military, and my mother was a stay-at-home mom. My brother, Carl, was born a year into their marriage. I was born about four and half years later. By then, something happened in my parents' marriage, and since then my life felt like a turbulent emotional rollercoaster ride. My out-of-control life began when I was about four years old; that is as far back as I can remember. Yes, the downward spiral of events started then because I recall being in pre-kindergarten.

My daddy had some personal issues that caused him to abuse drugs and alcohol. To say the least, the devil had his mind. Since my family did not know how to deal effectively with our problems, it allowed room for the enemy and his troops to create a lot of heartache, division and devastation to our family unit. I did not know then what I know now about my daddy's problems. I do not blame him anymore for the past hurts we endured. Today, I have nothing but love and compassion for him because I understand why he had to leave us for a while or was it the other way around? Maybe we had to leave him.

I will share an experience that I had when I was about four years old. You will begin to understand why I had difficulties communicating. You may even see the connection between the struggles I had in my relationships, especially in my romantic relationships with men, and the internal stress it caused me. To be even more transparent, you may notice how the enemy gained access to me. Then you will begin to understand why going back to this place, the place where it all started, was necessary.

I had to go back to face my demons so that I could tell them in their face how much of a liar they are, as well as show them that I am no longer afraid of them. You see, I had to trample over them so I could release my fears and walk with God towards my destiny. Before I could travel back to that place in time, I had to do some heart work exercises. God had to release me from the spirit called pride and its legions of corruptive friends like rejection, anger, and envy to build up my confidence so that I could transform into the person that God created me to be. It was necessary for this to happen first so that I could discover and understand who I am in Christ and not feel shamed or condemned about my past.

During my heart work exercise, God had me reading a lot of scripture and books. I wrote in a journal throughout the process too. I prayed and meditated on the Word of God more than ever. I had to release worldly things that I became accustomed to, like the type of music I listened to and the television shows or movies that I watched. I had to practice the ways of Jesus, such as acting in love, fighting for my peace of mind, and repenting when I missed the mark.

This process was not easy. I felt like I was in what I termed "spiritual boot camp" because I had to retrain my mind to operate in the laws that God set forth. God was breaking me down so that he could build up the Christ-like character buried deep within me. He was transforming me into the beautiful person that I am today. It was not an easy feat because I had to erase and wipe out from my mind all of the worldly standards, religious rules, and the viewpoints of others that went against my divine design that restricted me from living my purpose.

Now think about the resistance, the pull, and the tug-of-war battles you have when you are trying to resist an urge or temptation to do something you know is not in your best interest to do. You know that feeling of inner turmoil that sometimes spills out when you feel frustrated or tired. It takes blood, sweat, and tears to hold back from giving in to Satan's schemes. However, the more you practice it, the easier it becomes. The practice then becomes a habit that eventually develops your character. It is similar to a person beginning to work out or train to develop his muscles or to improve his quality of life. The more he works out, the more it becomes part of his routine. To develop a routine or habit, you must do some internal work, which is the training of your mind so that you can remain motivated to keep working out. When your internal programming is on the good channel, the results from the workout will begin to show outwardly.

Throughout my training, God showed me how Satan operates. I was able to identify his tactics. It helped me to resist giving in to his evil plots. The more I practiced resisting Satan, the better choices I made, and the outcome began to show in the physical realm.

Becoming transparent, showing others your pain, shame, hurts and disappointments that lie buried deep within the depths of your soul is not as simple as it seems. It takes work to become transparent because society has trained us to keep all of the bad, ugly details quiet. I struggled initially with sharing my story because of those reasons, but what I discovered was that it was another one of Satan's tricks to try to keep me quiet. If he can keep you feeling guilty, ashamed or hurt about your past, then, of course, you will not share it with others. God wants to heal you by releasing you from the emotional baggage that you are carrying.

Let us look at how the enemy found my open door and entered. When I came to know my dad, he was a full-fledged druggy and alcoholic. My mom worked, and daddy took or stole the money to feed his habits. He would do weird and crazy things that embarrassed me, like yelling and cursing at the top of his lungs outside at no one in particular. He abused my mother physically and verbally. I remember one time he threw a chair at my mom during one of their fights, and the bottom leg of the chair cut through her arm. That injury caused us to take a trip to the emergency room. I remember my mother suffering from bruises, cuts, and black eyes.

I even saw my dad smoke crack in the bedroom. He used a Colt 45 beer can as his crack pipe. He cut a hole on the top side of the can, dropped the drug inside and put a lighter underneath the can as he inhaled the crack fumes through the top opening of the can. Imagine being a four-year-old little girl seeing your daddy kill his brain cells and beating up on your mother. Yep, what a beautiful world I lived.

My daddy's drug addiction led him to do dangerous and illegal things to feed his bad habit. It often got him into trouble with the law. I mean my dad shot a man, and although, by the grace of God the man did not die, my dad had to serve some time behind bars. On one occasion after being released from jail, he was on probation and put on house arrest. Another one of his stipulations for being out of jail was that he had to take random drug tests. He was so addicted to drugs that he allowed the neighborhood drug dealer to talk him into drinking a cup of bleach and water so that he could continue purchasing and using drugs while on house arrest. So he did. He bought and used drugs while he was on house arrest. He also drank bleach and water every week to clean out his system of any drugs so that he could pass the drug test. When he finally did get tested for drugs the examiner could not pick up any traces of anything in his system. I mean no drugs or nothing else could be detected. Needless to say, he found a way to beat the drug test to continue feeding his bad habit. Hearing about my daddy's past mischief and also seeing his reckless and destructive behavior, I can see that God truly had a hand in his life because he should have been dead by now or at least in prison serving a life sentence. I can happily report that daddy is now honoring the Lord and living a healthy life. But, we had some dark times back before he repented and began serving the Lord.

Here is how it sounded when my dad and mother fought. "Curt, No! Stop, the children are watching."

"Shut up you *****. Where is the money?"

"Curt, I don't have any money."

"You are lying, *****."

A storm of punches would then plummet my mother's face and body. A streamline of obscenities crushed her spirit. My mom, brother and I tried to escape, but he kept us inside. All I heard were cries, screams, and loud sounds! My brother attempted to help momma, but he was not strong enough. I retreated more and more into myself. I crawled up in a corner and cried. I was emotional. I could not handle it, so after each fight, I would retreat to that safe place inside of me and cry out to God. The pain I felt engulfed me. My heart broke with each blow and after each string of curse words.

After each disappointment, my sense of love, safety, and trust began to fade, and I was left feeling hopeless, empty and afraid. My identity and my confidence were shattered like broken glass. My hopes and dreams were crushed. My family was destroyed. I was a young girl out in the world alone because my family was torn apart. I retreated further and further inside of myself. My voice became nearly inaudible, only a soft whisper when I spoke. The enemy had me. I was a little girl who was lost and confused because my parents had so many issues that even they could not protect me. You see, that is how Satan and his troops found an opening door to gain access to me. Yep, he caused the head of my family, my daddy, to go insane, which caused him to strike and ridicule his wife, my momma. Then that devil came after me.

My mom, brother and I lived in a fearful abusive home until I was seven years old. Momma could not take the abuse any longer, so we left and moved in with my maternal grandparents. When we lived with daddy, we had some dark, bad, and ugly moments. I call them moments because that is how long it seemed to last when it occurred. Then, things would get okay again because our extended family members would quickly step in to support us.

My mother had to raise my older brother and me as a single parent. Even though we did not have much money, I do not remember going without our basic needs met. Momma always kept our electricity on, provided us with a home, and food to eat. I almost received everything that I wanted that was within reason. My mom's parents, my Granddad Berry and Grandma Madea, helped us financially and emotionally.

When we lived with Madea and Grandad Berry, there was already a house full of people living there with them. My grandma's younger sister passed away in her sleep. She had young children, so Madea, their aunt, became their guardian and took care of them. My mom's side of the family is originally from a very small southern town. It is one of those small towns where it seems like everyone knows one another or are related to one another in some way.

My Grandma Madea moved to Florida looking for a better life. At the time, she had only one child, my mom. Let me tell you about my Madea. She is very similar to Tyler Perry's Madea. No offense to Tyler Perry but my Madea is, even more, hilarious and stronger than his character. She is like a loan shark; we all go to her when we need some money. If you owe her money, believe me, she is running a tab and calculating the interest. She has a way of never letting you forget that you owe her money so that you make every effort to pay her back. I do not know what the family would do without her, which is why I pray that God grants her healing and good health as often as I think of her.

Madea is the rock of the family. She is the only person who is still alive out of her immediate family, making her the matriarch of our family tree. Her father, mother and two sisters are all deceased. My grandma is hard working and ambitious. Altogether, she birthed three children: my mother and my two uncles. She raised them as a single parent. One of my uncles, my Uncle Bobby, I never really got a chance to know because he was shot and killed when I was four years old.

Granddad Berry and Madea met when her children were entering their teenage years and early adulthood. They eventually married a month after I was born. Berry accepted Madea's children, grandchildren, nieces, and nephews as his own. He is the only male that has been a consistent, dependable figure in all of our lives, so for that reason, we do not consider him a stepparent. He is our dad, granddad, and uncle, point blank period.

Although my family had some ugly and dark moments, I remember having a fun childhood. My dad's family was just as much a part of our life as my mom's side of the family. My dad's mom, Grandma Darlene, had eight children that she raised as a single parent as well. She married her deceased husband, Paul, when her children were adults. I remember attending their wedding when I was about five years old at their church.

My Granddad Paul, who I call Pa, is the only granddad I ever knew on my dad's side of the family. He also became the father of my grandma's children. Calling someone a stepparent or step grandparent was not something my family accepted on either side. When you became a part of our family, you were family, period, and there were no questions or explanations needed.

My Pa and Grandma modeled the Christian way of living for the family. They always attended church and lived a humble lifestyle. They are decent, church-going, loving folks.

When I was a young girl, Pa and Grandma's house was the place to be on holidays or special occasions. It was always some form of fun and hilarious entertainment. My aunts and uncles are all funny people, and they love to fight. We did not have or need HBO to see a comedy show or a boxing match. My aunts were fierce fighters. If my dad tried to fight my mom in front of them, they would all help my mom fight him, and I heard they would win, too. I had so many cousins to play with whenever my brother and I went over there, especially girl cousins, that I did not want to go home. I always found an auntie's house to visit for the day or to stay overnight so that I could play with my cousins. I longed for female companionship, so I looked up to my girl cousins. At home, I often played with my Barbie dolls, and they eventually became my friends. I was the youngest, and my brother was outside often playing with his buddies, so I was left inside to play by myself. I remember praying and wishing for a sister growing up so that I could have someone to talk to and play with who would understand me. God has sent me several sisters, and although we are not biological sisters, we are linked through Christ.

On the outside, I had a great childhood, and it appeared as if all was well with my family and me. When my mom, brother and I moved in with mom's parents, life began to brighten up for us. Daddy would come by sometimes to see us. He would take me on rides back to our old neighborhood to hang out with his friends. I loved my daddy. I was my daddy's little girl. Even though he had some issues, they did not stop me from loving him. I understood why my daddy and momma could not live together, and I accepted it. It was best for all us.

Chapter Three

Discovering and Destroying Your Purpose: The decisions and choices that turn you away from following your heart's desires

"Sir, didn't you sow good seed in your field? Where did the weeds come from? An enemy did this, he replied." --Matthew 13:27-28

My relationship with my dad began to fade when I realized that my daddy did not do things for us like Rudy's dad, Dr. Huxtable, did for his family. If you are familiar with the TV show called, The Cosby Show, then you can relate to this next statement. Back in the day, The Cosby Show was the television series that gave the world a positive outlook on the African-American family. It was the family that every little black girl wished and hoped they had. After I had compared my dad to Heathcliff Huxtable, I made a decision that caused me a lot of heartache and pain. I began to despise him for not being like the dad I saw on TV. As I grew older, I continued to compare my father to other men who I felt were great fatherly role models, like Heathcliff Huxtable, and the more I did that, the deeper into sin I fell.

As far back as I can remember, I was an avid reader. I always had my head in a book. I read nonfiction books, biographies, and autobiographies that shared the life stories of great people like Dr. Martin Luther King, Rosa Parks, and Thomas Jefferson. You see how God works. He was designing my paths by placing books about great people in my hands, yet the devil used it against me to trick my mind. However, when God's hands are in the midst, it does not matter what tricks the devil attempts because God will prevail every time.

I was reading about people who started movements that helped to change the lives of many individuals for the better. I read beautiful stories based on people who faced many adversities, conquered their enemies and became victorious. Their life stories gave me hope and inspiration, and I am sure they did the same for you too. These courageous individuals uplifted people and produced bold changes in the world that we all still reap benefits from today. I wanted to become just like them. I wanted to help better people's lives. Do you see the connection?

Yes, to heal from your past and present situation so that you can begin to operate in your purpose, you must go back in time to the place and time where the hurt began. To figure out your real identity, heal and build up your confidence, you have to go back to where the hurt entered into your subconscious mind. Here is the tricky part: Do not stay stuck there. To go back to the place where it all began, you must allow God to prepare you for it. As I mentioned earlier, it takes training and preparation to face your demons. Allow me to reveal some details as to how the enemy operates.

After seeing and reading about people at their greatest, I compared them to my dad and then I made a very dangerous decision. I decided to stop loving my father because I felt he was undeserving of my love, and he did not measure up to the fathers I had read about or had seen on television. I felt that he was an embarrassment to our family because he was not living up to the potential that I felt he was capable of becoming.

My final straw was when my daddy made me a promise that he did not keep, once again. I had enough of the broken promises. I felt like he should have at least made the effort to make sure that his baby girl was safe, protected and loved. I decided that it was the last time he would let me down.

After I made my decision and acted upon it, I noticed his visits became less frequent. Then I heard that he had moved to Daytona, Florida, about an hour away from us, and he had a new girlfriend. Hearing the news about his new life did not bother me at all because I had removed him from my life and shut him out of my heart.

Little did I know that removing my love for him, as well as the love for others who I felt disappointed me throughout the years, would cause me to experience so much more heartache and pain. Instead of dealing with my hurts, I learned to ignore them and remove the person who I felt hurt me from my life by cutting off the very existence of them from my mind. All the while, I had a hurricane of emotions swirling around inside of me.

My dad was the first man who I felt had rejected me. Rejection is a hard pill to swallow. It brings forth other destructive feelings like loneliness, resentment, and worthlessness. I battled with all of those emotions, plus more. I felt that my dad did not love me enough to fight for me, and of course, I felt that he should have fought harder to overcome his issues for me. I was his baby girl. I needed him to love me, be there for me, care for me, and to keep his promises. I needed him for everything. I felt disappointed, ashamed, and exposed.

I chose to deal with my hurt and disappointments by shutting people or situations out of my life and heart. Whenever my dad would come to visit, he received a frigid welcome from me. I became the ice queen when daddy came around. I intentionally left the room or house when he visited, so a conversation, or a relationship with him, was nonexistent.

This behavior went on until I was about thirty years old. Let us do the math: I was about eleven when I cut him off. So, that adds up to be about twenty years of not loving and speaking to my dad. Whoa, that is a long time! I was only hurting myself by hating him. The Bible says, "Anyone who attacks his father or his mother must be put to death (Exodus 21:15)." I was not attacking my dad physically, but I was sucker punching him with my indifference, and that can be a gut wrenching and painful blow to someone who loves you. I would not be surprised if my behavior and bad attitude caused my dad to suffer more pain and grief than I am sure he was already experiencing.

There is a quote I have heard people say that resonates in my being as truth. "Hurt people hurt other people." The cycle of pain continues until someone breaks it by taking a new and better approach to dealing with the issue. I know now that my dad was hurting, but back when I was a young girl, I did not know it. I took my hurt personally, and I avenged myself. I was disrespectful, arrogant, and rude towards my dad. I was disobedient and unforgiving. Ephesians 6:1 & 3 reads, "Children obey your parents in the Lord, for this right… that it may go well with you and that you may enjoy long life on the earth." If you believe in God and his Word, then know that my next statement is true. I was killing myself. I was setting up my murder.

The devil could not do anything to me. Cleverly, he made me feel like I was worthless, and that negative perception is what caused me to hate or mistreat others who I felt hurt me. The conniving devil has a way of omitting very relevant information that will help you to understand why someone may have handled a situation ineffectively or caused you to perceive a situation negatively. He places blinders over your eyes to make sure no light gets through because like the saying goes when you know better you do better, and of course, he does not want you to do better. He wants to keep you lacking and in need of his system so that you can keep relying on instant gratifications like drugs, alcohol, and sexual perversion to ease the pain that lies deep within. That is how he fooled me into falling into the deadly trap of holding unforgiveness in my heart, which caused me to react negatively towards others as well as myself.

The problem with those quick fixes, such as drugs and alcohol, is that they remove the pain temporarily. When the high wears off, it causes you to rely more on it to cope with life. This dependency results in you relying on Satan's system and less and less on God's system to make you feel alive. When I think back, I laugh at the devil because it is funny to me after realizing how he tried to trick and tempt me to remain on his deadly cycle. Luckily, God was with me through it all. His grace and mercy gave me time to correct my walk before I allowed Satan to lead me towards annihilation. The same goes for you too. As you are going through trials, God is with you every step of the way providing you with his unconditional love, grace and mercy to see you through each test.

As for me, I was not a rude or horrible child. I never gave my mother any significant problems. I made good grades and stayed out of the school principal's office. Overall, I was a decent child. I just directed those harmful behaviors toward my dad and others who I felt had wronged or hurt me in any way. I believe I was granted mercy before I repented and opened my heart up to accept God's calling for my life because I recognized the truth that Jesus died on the cross to save me from my sins when I was a young girl. Ironically, this happened around the same time when I decided to erase my dad from my life. I did not have a clue at that time about the Word of God, and I believed that Jesus was real because my heart told me that it was true.

I attended church when I was a young girl but not on every Sunday. I recall attending church with my dad's family sometimes. Pa and Grandma went to church every Sunday. They have many grandchildren, and we all would attend their church some Sundays and Bible school at times, too. I remember Grandma being so proud to see all of her grandchildren at church.

One particular Sunday, I went to church with my mother's friend. While sitting in church, I felt something in my heart when the pastor spoke that caused my heart to fill up with an overwhelming feeling of goodness. I do not know how to describe it other than the fact that it felt good, and it made me want to be a better person. Near the end of the service, the pastor asked the congregation to come to the front if they wanted to accept Jesus into their life. I was one of the people to walk to the front of the church to accept him into my life.

I remember sharing the experience I had in church that day with my Grandma and she told me, "Free, you do not have to only pray at night on your knees. You can pray standing, walking and all of the time." That is how I pray today. I pray everywhere I go. I pray in the car, in the bed, in the shower, and…you get the picture. I received my water baptism in that small church I visited, First New Zion Baptist Church.

After that experience, I felt a sense of safety and protection. I did not know scriptures, but I did know that Jesus was, and still is, real because I felt him in my heart, as I have felt so many times after that Sunday. I now understand that my earlier visits to church with my grandparents were preparing me for that very encounter with the Lord and Savior, Jesus Christ.

In Luke 23:34, Jesus said, "Father, forgive them, for they do not know what they are doing." Thank you, Jesus, for including me in that prayer request during my time of self-destruction, because honestly, I did not know what I was doing. I had no one to teach me at the level of understanding that I needed to know the truth that comes from the Word of God. My parents had their personal battles that they were dealing with, so they were incapable of teaching me. They were scrambling and trying to find the missing link just as much as I was, and like many of you are still today.

During my childhood and teenage years, I read the Bible but imagine a child reading the King James Version of the Bible. If you are familiar with that version of the Bible, then you will probably agree that the text can be hard for a young developing reader to follow. I needed a translated version of the Bible to gain a better understanding of the Word of God, and I discovered it at the age of nineteen when I joined another church. This particular church was bigger, and it had more members than the churches I was use to attending, which was smaller and had fewer members. The pastor preached and shared scriptures through the Good News version of the Bible. I was excited and on fire to read the Word. I had a Bible that I could finally read and understand. It was in plain English, Halleluiah!

The funny thing is that although I thought I was gaining an understanding, I was not on a spiritual level because I had not yet received the gift of the Holy Spirit. I was setting myself up for understanding though because I was searching for meaning, and when God sees you thirsty for him, he finds a way to send you a clear message.

Let me take you back to my middle school years. I ran into trouble. I started hanging with the wrong crowd, and I engaged in sex prematurely. Well, my momma found out about it, and I felt so inferior and ashamed. My mom is the strong, quiet type, so when she spoke with that particular firmness in her tone of voice, I listened. Then I would get myself together before I had to experience the fullness of her wrath. All my mother had to do to get me back in order was to give me "the look." You know that mean look adults give children when they are misbehaving. Well, my mom was the master at giving "the look," and raising her voice a tone higher than normal was enough to get me to conform to her commands.

I know she had to have done a lot of praying too because the sexual temptations just stopped. However, to ensure that I did not get pregnant, she took me to the clinic for a physical for birth control pills. I had to go to the clinic every three months for pill refills, and I disliked going there. I would beg her to stop taking me there. Mom had a way of disciplining me that made me see myself for who I was becoming, and that image would put me to shame. I made a promise to her that I would not get pregnant if she took me off the pill because I did not want to face the people in the clinic knowing my dirty secret. She eventually allowed me to get off the pill. My mom did not give my brother and me spankings, due to all the physical and mental abuse that we suffered at the hands of my dad. However, as I mentioned earlier, she had her way of disciplining us that made us obedient. Also, after the ordeal mom faced with our dad, we did not want to bring any additional pressure and stress in her life, so we tried our best to stay out of trouble.

What momma did not know was just how and when the bad seed of sexual behaviors planted inside of me. The seedling dropped in my spirit when I saw two grown-ups having sex when I was about six or seven years old. After seeing the act, I begin to desire to be touched like that too. An older male molested me when I was about eight years old. The person who touched me was about sixteen at the time. You can only imagine how messed up I was when it came to my sexuality. As I grew up, I despised sex and desired it at the same time! I only had sex to please the other person, because afterward I felt dirty and used. I was looking for love and sacrificing my temple. Thank you, Lord, for keeping me protected when I did not protect myself. I faced many adversities and hurts by the hands of men who could not love me the way I knew I deserved.

Throughout my life, it appeared as if men kept coming in and out of my life. After each one of them left me, I felt worthless than before. In my mind, I was defeated by love and damaged from the way I allowed them to use my body for their pleasure. I had become damaged goods, and I felt no one would ever be able to genuinely love me. I felt unloved and unworthy. It was as if I had the word "rejected" stamped in red across my forehead. I could relate to Miss Celie, the character in The Color Purple when she compared having sex with Mister to someone using the toilet on her.

Trust me when I say that if you see a person acting promiscuous, someone or something has planted an evil seed called sexual perversion into them. Please pray and intercede to request God's help immediately to come and save the individual. I know that my mother was my intercessor. I am sure that others were interceding and praying for me as well. I want you to know that I am forever grateful for each of the prayers I have received. I have forgiven myself for my past mistakes as well as those who hurt me. I know that they were hurting too. Yep, hurt people truly do hurt other people. Sadly, if you continue that cycle of pain, you will eventually hurt or kill yourself or someone else along the way.

The hopes and dreams I had as a young girl of one day helping others by boldly making my mark to help change the world's viewpoints, like the men and women I read about, were becoming even more nonexistent, leaving me just existing. I was passing the time by until I passed away. I thought, "My God, it has to be better than this, right?" Oddly, though my dad never abused me physically; however, witnessing the ordeal caused me to have many emotional torments that created problems in relationships, especially with men. I had deep trust issues rooted in me.

My mother, however, served as a positive role model of forgiveness for me. There were times when I became so angry with her for being so forgiving. You see, my mom endured a lot of pain and long suffering from the domestic violence she experienced. I am sure the outside bruises did not compare to the scars that she felt on the inside. She forgave my dad for everything, though. There were times when internally, I would be screaming at her to fight back. Now, I understand mom's approach. Forgiving others, as well as yourself, is the key that will open the door for God to enter and forgive you. In scripture, it states, "For if you forgive men when they sin against you, your heavenly Father will also forgive you (Matthew 6:14)." If you cannot find it in your heart to give mercy towards someone who has wronged you, then God will not give you mercy (see Matthew 18:21-35).

Forgiveness was yet another hard lesson for me to learn, but God came in and showed me the beauty in forgiving others. It holds the key to opening the door to receiving blessings. As I struggled with forgiving others due to holding on to my feelings of inadequacies, God told me that a king resides in me. The devil has no power over me anymore, so I needed to let my past mistakes, as well as the past mistakes of others, go. God said that because of Jesus' sacrifice, no more guilt or condemnation could hold me back from receiving the love that comes from Him (see Romans 8:39).

I am royalty! Any man who dares to approach me must serve the same God I serve. Romans 8:17 reads, "Now if we are children, then we are heirs—heirs of God and co-heirs with Christ if indeed we share in his sufferings so that we may also share in his glory." Thank you, Father, for loving me and showering me with your warm affection during the times I was blind and could not love myself.

Chapter Four

Satan's Vicious Cycle: The continuous destructive habits that lead to death

"The thief comes only to steal and kill and destroy." (John 10:10.)

After high school, I went to the university located in my hometown. I stayed on campus, but I came home to visit my mom on most weekends. Since I was attending college in town, I sometimes came home during the week and of course every holiday.

I received a full scholarship to college because of my high standing academics. I had mapped out a plan to graduate a year early from high school, after learning about the graduation requirements. Most of the people I hung out with were a year ahead of me, and I wanted to graduate with them. I did manage to graduate my junior year because I had earned all of the required credits and passed the high school exit exams.

After high school, the partying began. I partied like the artist Prince sang about in his song "1999." Although I did not take drugs, alcohol became my drug of choice. I got a hold of a fake ID, and I used it from age seventeen until I turned the legal age of twenty-one. To be honest, my first encounter with an adult nightclub was when I was about thirteen. I somehow managed to get into a club back when I was in middle school. Acting grown-up too soon is a sign that parents and guardians should intervene quickly because their child may need some deliverance like I needed the Lord to come quickly to rescue me.

I was so reckless using the fake ID that if someone had taken the time to ask me the name and address on the identification, I would not have given the correct information because I had not studied the information on the ID long enough to retain it in my memory.

Nonetheless, I was a smart goal-oriented college-going sister with no children. I was on my way to becoming an educator. My original major was business, but I later changed it to elementary education after discovering all of the higher-level math courses I was required to take to obtain a business degree. I did not want to stretch myself because I was getting by doing mediocre academic work. After I had realized I had to work harder than I was willing to do to obtain a business degree, I did not desire to pursue that career path anymore, so I set out to find something that was a little more befitting.

One day I visited my academic advisor to help me sort out my career choices. I shared with her that I wanted to become a child psychologist because I wanted to help hurt children. Ironically, at the time, I did not put myself in the category of being one of the hurt children that needed some healing because I was unaware of the tricks of the enemy. We agreed that it would be best for me to get a degree in a field that would land me a job in a related field. Then go to graduate school to obtain a master's degree in psychology. She shared with me that getting a master's level degree is the only way to secure a job in the psychology field. She advised me to major in education so that I can gain some experience working with children and earn a decent living. I went along with the plan and switched my major to education. I was not quite sure about becoming a teacher, but I did not have any other career options in mind.

I had a boyfriend during my first two years of college. He and I would attend church together sometimes, and it appeared that we were becoming very close. Until he began to share with me his desires to move to another city to work on establishing a career in music. I was sure that I was not going to leave my hometown to follow him. Not to mention the first two years of our relationship was long distance because he was attending school out of town. That relationship ended, and that was when I began to feel a tug in my heart to go towards God.

I was nineteen in my sophomore year of college when I felt the pull or conviction in my heart to return to church. I was headstrong and determined to make a good life for myself, but I didn't have a clue as to what I wanted out of life. I found a church and joined it. Up until this point, I had fooled myself into thinking that I was okay and that my dad's absence in my life did not affect me. However, shortly after joining the church, I encountered a man who diverted my attention away from God. I knew when I made the decision to date him that I was turning my back on God for man. I also knew that because of my decision that the relationship was doomed, but it did not stop me from trying. I was very infatuated with him. He was not the typical person I was used to dating. He was the bad boy that people warn young girls to stay away from because he will walk on your heart.

Well, I did not take heed to the warning. I stopped going to church and started partying again, but this time, it was different. I became, even more, careless and irresponsible than before. I did, however, manage to graduate from college with a degree in elementary education. I remember feeling so low at my graduation because I felt so unloved and unappreciated by him. The man who I thought I loved did not even show up for my graduation, nor did he think enough of me to buy flowers to congratulate me.

After college, I landed a teaching job. I felt this overwhelming sense of sadness on my first day at work. I was at my lowest when

I should have been at my highest. I had a college education and a career, but something was missing. I desperately wanted love by this man. I would bend over backward and jump through small hoops that I knew I could not fit through just to please him. I did things that were out of my character just to make him happy. All the while, I was getting nothing but empty words of affection in return.

Eventually, I got pregnant and later I terminated the pregnancy. I aborted my child because the man who impregnated me had rejected me. I felt that I could not live through another rejection period, so I gave in and aborted my pregnancy. The events after having the abortion were dark and lonely. By this time, I was living on my own, so I was able to hide my depression from my family.

My friends, however, saw the change in my mood and behavior, and they would drop by my apartment unexpectedly at times just to check up on me. I did not know why they were dropping by unannounced, but they eventually confided in me and told me that they were afraid that I would harm myself. I did attempt to kill myself at one time; however, in my mind, all I wanted to do was go to sleep so that the depressive thoughts of killing my baby would cease.

It was on Super Bowl Sunday 2003. I was lonely and grieving; I had taken so many Tylenol PMs to help me sleep that the recommended dosage did not have an effect on me any longer. I came up with a plan to help me get to sleep sooner. I decided to take six pills at once. Then drink shots of Tequila and chase it with Smirnoff Black coolers.

After ingesting all of the poison, I passed out on my living room couch. Something woke me up, and I vomited everywhere. I crawled into my room and climbed in my bed. As I was lying there, I thought to myself that I did not want to die alone. I managed to pick up the phone from the receiver, but I could not see the numbers clearly to make a call for help. Everything appeared blurry, and I blacked out again. I awakened again only to vomit the remainder of the poison out of my body. Next, I managed to get into the bathtub and turn on the shower. I let the water beat down on my skin until I felt myself gain some strength. I was so afraid, and it was at that moment I decided that I wanted to live and not die.

The next morning, I took a "sick day" from work so that I could clean up my home and rest from the previous night's events. That encounter with death scared me straight; at least, so I thought. I began to have a positive outlook on life and started making plans for my future. However, that only lasted about a month because I allowed the man whom I had gotten pregnant from to reenter my life again. The very first time we had sex after he and I ended our tumultuous relationship I got pregnant again. This time, I decided to keep my baby, and I did not care if he rejected me again or not. I was not going to kill another one of God's precious gifts of life. I remember during my dark moments after the abortion praying to God and asking Him to send my baby back to me. This pregnancy symbolized an answered prayer. Of course, the father of my child and I did not work things out, so my family, friends, and co-workers surrounded me with lots of love and support during my pregnancy. I felt strengthened and to this day, I believe that God sent my son to strengthen my faith and belief in Him. Before this ordeal, I did not have much faith or love in my heart for God or myself.

Although I had taken on the great task of motherhood, I still battled with insecurities that come with being a single parent. My son gave me a reason to believe and keep going during times in my life when I wanted to give up. I felt that no one would want to date me with a child. I was angry with his father because I felt rejected once again. Depression began to resurface, and I once again began to experience suicidal ideations.

I became reckless in my dealings with men. I would go out with men whom I knew I should have been running in the opposite direction. At one point, I did not care if I lived or died. If it had not been for my son, I probably would have allowed the enemy to keep pushing me towards death. Eventually, when my son was about two years old, I begin to feel better about life again. I even started looking for a home to purchase to recharge myself and get my life back on track. I went back to school to work on my master's degree in counseling education.

I eventually purchased a new home and car. My life was improving, and I was happy again. You see these were the times that I would have moments of clarity, but then a failed relationship would land me right back in what was becoming my favorite dark corner. I had developed some godly sense, so I knew where to turn when my thoughts became dark, or the burdens of life got too heavy. I would take out my Bible and read scriptures from the Book of Psalms. There were many nights when I slept with my Bible cradled close to my heart. I believed in God as a young child, but I was still immature in my spiritual development.

I was aimlessly wandering the world and wondering about God simultaneously. I did not understand the spiritual component of the church or the messages the preacher delivered. I would occasionally go to the church that my grandparents attended from time to time. I kept the deep-rooted insecurities locked inside of me. Therefore, I did not share much of my internal pain with anyone.

I know I would often leave people perplexed about me because I was not very talkative and open with people I did not know. I did not trust people easily. If I did not feel comfortable with you, then I would withdraw my presence, and my conversation was very limited. On the other hand, the people who I found that I could trust, I opened myself up to them. Once I felt a sense of safety with a person, I embraced them with love and shared some of myself with them, but they still did not know everything. I was unsuccessful in my love-relationship with men, but every other area in my life was on the up-and-up, or, at least, I thought they were.

Look at how the enemy operates. He used men to bring me down and the very first one he used against me was my dad. Wow! Do you see the pattern? Satan does not use new tricks. He sends the same culprit every time; it just takes on different faces.

Right around the time, I decided to give up dating and just focus on establishing friendships I met a man who appeared to be different from the men I dated in the past. I gave in to his advances, and we developed a relationship that eventually led to marriage. Well, what happened was I got pregnant, so we made a decision to go ahead and marry one another for this reason. I never envisioned myself ever getting married until we entertained the topic. It was at that moment that I began to want to be married. I started looking at wedding shows and buying the wedding magazines and books.

Sadly, I had a miscarriage soon after getting the ring. I grieved the death of my unborn child. I do not think my fiancé at the time understood what I was going through. Somewhere in the midst of my grief and the drama of the wedding planning, we disconnected.

In 2008, I once again got the urge to go back to church. I joined another church, but this church was different. I felt like I was at home when I attended church services. The bishop had a different style of preaching that was more like teaching. He did not yell and illicit fear in me like some of the pastors' messages I have heard. He referenced scriptures and broke down the meaning of words, which deepened my understanding of the Word of God. It felt like I was in bible school. The bishop seemed to come from a place of love, truth, and compassion when he spoke to his congregation about Jesus Christ. He appeared genuine, so I trusted him enough to sit back and listen. He kept my attention, and I kept going back to his church.

I eventually raised my hand during the altar call for rededication. I acquired the gift of the Holy Spirit during the new membership class back in August of 2008. Shortly after joining the church, I felt convicted to stop having sex and drinking. I stopped having sex and slowed my drinking down to occasional during our engagement period until I was married. During the relationship, there were signs indicating that we were not ready for marriage, but we kept pressing forward with our plans. One day, in church, the bishop gave a sermon about women in the church marrying men whom he did not know. He said that we were not bringing these men to the leaders of the church for counsel to help us determine if we were ready and equipped for marriage. He also stated that we would end up unhappily married or divorced. I knew I was one of the women he was speaking to, and to confirm it, my bishop and his family went on the same cruise my new husband, and I took for our honeymoon. Now, how strange is that!

I felt so ashamed because we had not received premarital counseling as my bishop encouraged us to do. I attempted to avoid my bishop and his family while on the cruise. I did not want to speak with him or acknowledge that I attended his church out of fear that he would recognize the fact that I was one of the women whom he was talking about in church that day. I remembered on the honeymoon feeling as if I had made a big mistake. I packed a book about how to succeed in a marriage for couples. I do not remember the title of the book, but I remember trying to read it with my new husband, but he was uninterested. He left the book and me in the room and went to one of the clubs on the cruise ships.

I loved my husband, but I was more so in love with the institution of marriage and the "happily ever after" ending. I felt empty. It felt like something was missing in our marriage and life but I could not figure out what, so I asked God to send me another child. I honestly thought a child would bring my husband and me closer together and fill the void that was swallowing our relationship. The night I made that request to God my husband, and I conceived a child.

I had a high-risk pregnancy, which caused me to go into premature labor. I was under undue stress at home and at work so my baby could not thrive inside of me. She arrived three months early. My precious baby lived in an incubator with small tubes attached to her fragile body for two months. She is a strong little girl, and I fell in love with her the moment of her conception. Watching her in such a fragile state was a traumatic experience. I kept praying that she would come home with nothing missing and nothing broken.

During the time my baby was in the hospital, I did not retreat inside as much as I did in the past. I went to church and stayed connected with my family and friends. My pastor was preaching a series about discovering your purpose. I purchased the book he used to teach the series. I even invited a few friends over to my house to discuss the lessons we learned about discovering our purpose. I wanted to follow my heart, and what was brewing in my heart was God. I wanted to align myself with Christ and follow him, but the distractions kept me wrapped in the world. I was on the fence with one foot hanging in the world and the other one hanging over in the holy land.

My precious Lila came home on February 15, 2010, with nothing missing and nothing, was broken. Praise God! Nevertheless, when she came home, the marriage began to crumble. I fought hard to save it. I focused more on the potential of how perfect things could be with us, but I lost sight of the present reality we faced. I will not go into the specific details of the demise of our relationship, but I can say this: We were unequally yoked. It opened the doorway for the enemy to attack us. My advice to couples is to seek counsel before you decide to marry, and to pray together always.

As for me, I was too spiritually immature to combat the attacks the enemy threw at us alone. My guess is that he was too. As they say, like attracts like. I held on, though, and I gave a good fight because I wanted to follow what the "Good Book" says you must do in marriage. I received counseling at my church to help me during my grief moments so that I could deal with divorce in a healthy way.

I was furious and bitter during the divorce process. I blamed my ex-husband for the demise of our relationship and lashed out at him terribly. I was so angry with him for not fighting to keep his family intact, but like Psalm 127 states, "Unless the Lord builds the house, its builders labor in vain." The Lord was not the builder of our marriage, so our foundation collapsed and we failed.

After the anger had subsided, I felt embarrassed by my behavior towards my ex. I was a Christian; nonetheless, I was immature in my walk with Christ, but I still held myself accountable for my actions. After viewing the errors of my ways, the guilt and condemnation started to play on my psyche. I felt obligated to hold on to the marriage due to the scriptures I had been reading about marriage and divorce. I was fighting to live according to the Word, but I was still battling with the temptations of the world and the demons that I held within me. Eventually, I released and let go of the man and the marriage in hopes that we both could heal.

After the divorce, I still suffered lots of grief. I dealt with an array of emotions. I felt guilty, ashamed, exposed, vulnerable and hurt. I kept relating to myself as divorced. It was as if I became the image of divorce and I exemplified every negative aspect of it. To make things clearer, I felt like a failure. It was as if I was on a stage and the whole world was viewing my performance and pitying me at the same time.

My counselor at my church pointed out the fact that I kept identifying myself as divorced and she said to me that being divorced does not determine my identity. After that revelation, I begin to work harder to discover my purpose in life as well as my identity. I was tired of being in the dark and straddling the fence of life and death. Yes, I was married, and the marriage ended, but the person I am is not a representation of divorce. The quest for discovering my purpose started up again when I realized that I am not nor will I ever be an image of death.

Chapter Five

The Fight: The closer you get to revelation the more the enemy attacks

"Finally, let no one cause me trouble, for I bear on

my body the marks of Jesus." (Galatians 6:17)

A few months after the divorce finalized, I made the decision to move out of my mother's house and start my life over with my children. I even began to date, however, after a while I realized that it was too soon and very much a distraction for me to open myself up to a romantic relationship. I continued dating, even after I knew I should have ended it, just to save face and not appear to be a lonely person, even though I was very much alone.

I was still trying hard to seek out God's purpose for my life, and I wanted so desperately to stop sinning. I wanted to live a life of peace, harmony, joy and love like God promises his children (see Galatians 5:22-23). The more I fought for that lifestyle, the more the enemy attacked me. I pressed in hard to the Word of God because I felt in my spirit that the devil did not want me to get to that place of peace and love in Christ Jesus because he knew his days with me would be over. The Bible says that the enemy comes to kill, steal and destroy, and that is what he was attempting to do to me (see John 10:10).

During the year of the divorce proceedings, I began to develop pain in my joints and an overall sick feeling that eventually landed me in my primary doctor's office. The symptoms I experienced were pain and swelling in my joints, such as knees, elbows, and hands. I also had low-grade fevers and extreme fatigue. I had the malaise feeling. You know when you feel like you are not well, and can't quite identify the cause, but you know that something is not functioning well in your body.

After running a series of tests, my doctor discovered that I had lots of inflammation, so she referred me to a rheumatologist for further testing. The rheumatologist diagnosed me with having a medical condition called Rheumatoid Arthritis, also known as RA. RA has the potential of deforming and disfiguring the parts of the body where joints are prevalent, like the hands and feet. RA can lead to other major complications, such as lung disease and cancer.

The medication used to treat RA can also become life-threatening, so the rheumatologist had to monitor me carefully. However, I was not satisfied with my treatment options, and I confided my dissatisfaction to one of my sorority sisters, and she referred me to try another rheumatologist.

My new rheumatologist or "rheumy" ran some more tests, and she confirmed the original diagnosis of RA. I started a new treatment regime, and she carefully monitored my progress. However, I was not getting better, but worse, as I began to develop skin rashes. I went to a dermatologist who blew it off as eczema and acne. I did not agree with that diagnosis. I kept getting worst, and my rheumatologist could not get a handle on the inflammation. The irritable, prickly and itchy rashes began to show up on my face, hands, and chest. Also, I still had constant inflammation that caused stiffness and pain in just about every joint in my body.

On this one particular visit, I showed the doctor the rashes, and she became very concerned and alert. She referred me back to the dermatologist for further investigation. This time, I went to a different dermatologist within the same practice.

On the day of the dermatologist visit, I had an RA flare-up. The term "flare-up" is used when the RA symptoms are present and active in your body. The flare-up symptoms I experienced in addition to pain and inflammation were fever and extreme fatigue. I could barely walk that day. I felt miserable and tired from the consistent flare-ups and skin issues. When I pulled into the parking lot of the dermatologist's office, I sat in my car and prayed that God would give the dermatologist wisdom and insight so that she could make the right diagnosis.

The medication I was on for RA was not working for me. During the times that I felt the most horrible, I kept my mind on Jesus. He was the medication that was sustaining me up to this point because the prescribed medicine I had been taking was not alleviating the symptoms in my body. However, I felt strong in my spirit, and I held on to this blind faith. My body just needed to get in alignment with what my mind felt.

Before I developed any of the RA symptoms, I encountered a spiritual woman of God, and she told me to read the scripture about the woman with the issue of the blood (see Mark 25-34). How ironic is that! It was that scripture that I focused on as I pressed in and asked Jesus to deliver healing to my body during the battle with RA symptoms. After the prayer request in the car that day, the Lord answered it immediately, and I began to see the miracles manifest in the physical realm.

When I entered the examination room, the dermatologist went straight into action. She was very observant and asked very specific questions that led me to feel very confident in her abilities. She collected some of my skin to run a biopsy to test for Lupus. Her suggestion shocked me, but I had a feeling that she was close to finding out the source of my issues. I shared with her that I have already gotten two doctors to confirm that the joint pain, fever, and malaise symptoms are from RA, so I could not have developed Lupus. She began to share with me that autoimmune diseases can overlap each other, and it is possible to have more than one autoimmune diagnosis.

Next, she instructed her nurse to perform the biopsy. She cut out a circular sample of my skin from my left arm near my elbow to examine. She left me in the office with the nurse after stating that she wanted to see me back in her office in four weeks. I received instructions on how to treat the wounded area and two prescriptions for steroid-based creams to begin applying on the problem skin areas.

I walked out of the office feeling slightly broken because I faced the possibility of battling two chronic medical conditions. When I got into my car and digested the events that occurred in the office—the skin biopsy and the doctor's suggestion of Lupus—I had an emotional sobbing moment. I cried out to God and asked him, "Am I dying," because I kept getting more bad news about my health status.

I called my mother to tell her the latest news, but she did not answer the phone. I then called my grandma Madea. I was sobbing as I gave her the update from my dermatologist visit. She reminded me of two very important people who depend on me, my children, and that I could not die and leave them.

Immediately after she gave me that declaration, I had an overwhelming feeling that she was right and that I was going to live. The Lord used Madea to reveal a powerful and profound purpose that triggered me into making a life-changing decision. On July 3, 2012, I choose to live and not die. God then turned my attention towards my two small babies, and I began to remember the night of each of their conceptions. I knew the exact day of my children's conception because I prayed and asked God to send them to me. I always knew that He sent them to me for a particular purpose, but the events and distractions that happened in my life blinded my view and blocked my hearing.

God's hand delivered me both of my children during times when I was at low points in my life, to breathe life into me. God trusted me with His babies so I could train them in the Word of God so that they would not depart from Him (see Proverbs 22:6). I decided to live so that I could live up to God's expectation and teach my children about the Father, the Son, and the Holy Spirit.

During the conversation, Madea instructed me to pray, and she told me that she loved me. Love and support wrapped its arms around me, and I felt God's presence. I felt immersed in His Holy Spirit. I felt renewed with a firm stance, and I refused to go to that place of darkness that I retreated to in times of disappointment. The Lord answered my prayers and on that day my life, as I had known it, changed.

In the parking lot outside of the dermatologist's office, I had discovered one of my purposes. The first purpose he showed me was that he blessed me with two beautiful children to love and teach them the ways of the Lord. Wow! He chose me for them and them for me so that I could teach them about the life of Jesus and receive God's promises. He also showed me that he had been with me all along. I felt the presence of the Lord that day, and I let go of the world and grabbed hold of Jesus' hand. From that day to the present, I stand firm in my belief that Jesus is the only way to reach the Kingdom of Heaven. Jesus came down from Heaven and delivered me from out of the belly of the beast so that I could live out the purpose-filled life God planned for my children and me.

He revealed to me that I received healing a few months prior when I activated my faith and touched his cloak as I meditated and believed in His Word. I felt healed in my spirit. The more I focused on my healing, the better my body began to feel. I still took the medications my doctor ordered, but it was not until I activated my faith and allowed Jesus to lead my life that I began to feel better. The enemy saw I was beginning to feel better and stronger, so he then magnified the rash I had to try to deter my healing process.

After four weeks, I went back to the dermatologist to get the results from the biopsy. The results came back as a possible connective-skin disease, such as lupus or dermatomyositis. I took the results back to my rheumatologist who then ran some more tests. Two days after my visit, the rheumy called me to share my lab results with me. I got my answer in two days. I am pointing this out to share just how quickly God works when you choose to follow Jesus. The findings were conclusive to having developed a connective-skin disease called dermatomyositis.

Dermatomyositis is also an autoimmune disease that has the same symptoms as RA, but it attacks the muscles. A skin rash characterizes it. I remember feeling a sense of relief when she told me the prognosis because although I had begun to feel better, I was hopeful that she could place me on the right treatment plan. By this time, I had less joint pain, and the malaise feeling had subsided. I still was battling the irritable and unattractive rashes. The same medicine prescribed for RA is the same medication that is used to combat dermatomyositis. I just needed an extra boost of one of the prescribed medications to kick my body into gear. I contribute the upgrade in my health to the healing I obtained through my faith.

By the time I got the results back from my rheumy, I did not care what other tests she or any other doctor ran on me because I knew that I had received healing, and, therefore, I ordered my body to get in alignment. I began to pray for the removal of the ugly and itchy rashes from my body. My God is not a God, who will lie. If He says that you receive healing because of your faith, then without a doubt I knew that I had received it.

Whenever the devil would try to trick me into thinking I was sick, and the rash was not going away, I focused on the truth more than the facts. Yes, it is a fact that I received a diagnosis of having a medical condition. Yes, I have symptoms of the illness, but even those symptoms are lessening. Those are all facts, but the truth of the matter is that I have received my healing from those medical conditions because Jesus told me so.

Within two months after receiving the prognosis of dermatomyositis, I felt healing manifest itself in my body. The rashes disappeared and the RA flare-ups; hmmm, let me think. Well, after thinking about it, I have not had any flare-ups that lasted longer than a few hours, in months. In the past, I had flare-ups that lasted all day and every day for about a year. Praise God! During that time, my body felt beaten down, whipped, and worn out from all of the pain and sicknesses that tried to cripple and overtake me. I am still taking medication, but everything in me believes that one day I will be off all medications and will be symptom-free.

Medicine, to me, serves as a bandage or covering until your real healing manifests itself in the natural, or the Lord may use it to give you the quality of life that you deserve. If you are taking medicine prescribed by a physician, then I encourage you to follow your doctor's orders but continue holding on to faith until your doctor orders you to stop taking medication. God created doctors and medicine for a purpose, so we must remain obedient until He instructs the doctor to move you off the regimen. Always use your discernment and seek out another opinion when the Holy Spirit prompts you. The devil is very tricky. He will trick your mind into believing that you are dying by sending you all of these different medical prognoses and symptoms. Yes, it is a fact that your physical body will not last forever, but the truth is that when you are in the body of Christ, you can live beyond the medical prognosis and defeat the odds.

It is God's spirit that dwells inside of believers and allows us to continue to live even after our fleshly body dies. When God lives inside of you, you will not and cannot depart this earth without fulfilling His purpose for your life unless you choose not to answer His call. I am here to testify to you that once you accept the trinity, God the Father, Christ the Son and the Holy Spirit, you will not die but will continue to live!

Chapter Six

The Life-Changing Decision: Changing your heart and mind so that it resembles Christ

"Create in me a pure heart, O God, and renew a steadfast spirit within me." (Psalm 51:10)

Let me take you back to the day I left the dermatologist's office on July 3, 2012. I was in my car crying, feeling a little defeated and wondering where I went wrong. I asked God "Is this it for me? Am I dying?" Then a vision of my two beautiful children came to me, and a surge of strength entered my body. Immediately afterward I felt a shift occur in my thoughts about my health and my mind become stronger than ever. I began to see glimpses of what I was destined to become flash quickly before my eyes. It was then that I became determined to live.

My life as I knew it has not been the same since the day I grabbed hold of Jesus' hand and leaped over the fence that I had been straddling. The fence that I am referring to is that middle or gray area that believers sometimes get stuck on while holding on to worldly behaviors and sinful thoughts, yet loving and believing in God. It is confusing, huh? Yes, this is how the enemy sets us up for failure.

It was not until I decided to live when God began to identify who I truly was and why He created me. He tried to show me the way, but I was too distracted and beaten down to hear or even see His attempts. I was stuck in the gooey quicksand of the world, sinking slowly into the underworld. To make it clearer, you cannot love God and the devil too. In 1 Kings 18:21 God's prophet Elijah said, *"How long will you waver between two opinions? If the Lord is God, follow him: but if Baal is God, follow him."* Jesus said, "No one can serve two masters." (Mathew 6:24.)

When you attempt to serve God and the world, it causes confusion, chaos and all types of drama to line up at your doorstep. The drama (legions of spirits) knocks and waits for entrance into your home so that they can get their turn at trying to wipe out your existence. They want to keep you from becoming the person God destined you to be.

If you are stuck in that middle area that I call quicksand it will slowly but surely devour you, or maybe you simply do not believe in the Lord and Savior, and that is why you feel so unfulfilled. You know it feels like something is missing in your life, but you cannot put your finger on it. That feeling makes you keep searching for fulfillment, so you find yourself going from one relationship to another relationship, switching jobs or careers, or beginning but never finishing new projects. Maybe, you have just settled because you have given up hope that maybe there is something better here for you. Does this sound familiar to your situation or someone you know?

Well, I can testify from my experience, and I know it to be true that Jesus Christ is the only way to our Father, God in Heaven. His free and supernatural gift of the Holy Spirit is real (see John 14). If you want to discover that missing piece of you so that you can heal, learn who you are and find out your purpose for being here on this earth, then you must accept Jesus into your heart. Now, take His hand and journey along with Him to discover your greater self.

I will demonstrate how quickly God works when you allow Jesus to take the lead in your life. For so long I had accepted Christ as my Lord and Savior; however, I did not understand His purpose. I believed in God, and I prayed relentlessly. I even felt a level of intimacy and connection with Him in my early childhood and early adult years. I kept on sinning and doing what I wanted to do all while negating the commandments telling me what thou shall not do. I continued lying, fornicating, drinking excessively, and partying, all while having suicidal ideations. To state it simply, I was ignoring

God point-blank, period. I even committed an act of murder when I aborted my first child.

I was a self-destructive mess, killing myself with every step that I took without accepting the Lord's way. I was comparable to an adulterer because I was holding on to my friendship with the world. Therefore, I was an enemy of God (see James 4:4). I was wandering aimlessly around as if He did not have a purpose for my being here. I even questioned my existence. What is the point of living if all I feel is disappointment? Why am I so unhappy even when everything around me appears to be okay? Why am I here?

The irony about me inquiring about my existence was that deep down inside, at the core of my soul, I felt as if I was destined to become someone great. I was never satisfied with the status-quo lifestyle, but I was living it. I was miserable. I thought that my greatness would never form. I felt trapped inside my soul. I was looking for a way to escape from myself so that I could be free to develop into this great being that I felt I was destined to become.

I did not know the path to take to get there because the majority of people around me were living the life that I was trying to escape. Everywhere I looked I saw sinful and adulterous behaviors. I was looking for God, but I could not find Him in the lifestyles of most of the people around me. My hope was steadily declining toward the depths of Hades. I blindly made decisions that caused me to incur crippling emotional and physical pain.

It was not until I began studying the Word of God daily and believing in Jesus' ability to heal and lead me to our Father God that I finally got it! God loves me so much that He created a Son in his image to teach, model, and show me exactly how to live eternally. He wanted me to heal so He sent his son Jesus to heal me from all of my hurts, pains, and sicknesses. He wants me to seek Him daily so that I can understand my purpose and live in shalom—complete peace. God wants me to share my story, the lessons I learned and the truth about Jesus Christ so that you too can accept His hand and heal from the internal sickness that is controlling your mind. God wants you to discover your real identity and purpose. God does not wish to leave anyone behind and neither do I.

One of my heart's desires is for you to enter the Kingdom of Heaven right along with me. I know the torturing and tormenting slow death that you will experience if you do not accept Jesus' hand and believe in His Word. I know this to be true because I experienced it. In Proverbs 1:32 it is written, "For the waywardness of the simple will kill them and the complacency of fools will destroy them." I know that Jesus came and saved me from the belly of the beast. Yes, God came down from Heaven to deliver me from the Hades I was in right here on earth.

On July 3, 2012, when I took hold of Jesus' hand, I activated my faith in His healing authority; I gave Him full control over my life. I was finally over the fence and out of the quicksand. I landed on Holy grounds, and I was so overjoyed and excited to honor and glorify the Lord. I felt like a child playing in the snow. I imagined myself rolling around on Holy grounds making snow angels. I was so happy, and that emptiness feeling dissipated. I continue to give thanks and praise to God for sending His Son, Jesus to save my old, wretched soul because without his undying love and compassion I would have surely perished.

When the Lord heals you, he does not just heal you from your present illness or pain. He feels you from the inside out, which means he takes you all the way back to that place where it all began. For me, it all started when I was four years old when I witnessed my father abuse my mother and drugs. The emotional abuse I endured caused me to make some unwise decisions, which would have led me to die a horrendous death. Thank you, God, for sending your angels to help guide me towards your shining light.

Chapter Seven

Earthly Angels: People whom God assigns to plant or water His seed

"I planted the seed, Apollos watered it, but

God made it grow." (1 Corinthians 3:6)

The first angel He sent me was my uncle's first wife, Hillary whom I call by her middle name Nicole. I met her when I was four years old, and we instantly clicked. I admired and adored my Auntie Nicole. She was educated, beautiful, young and free. Sometimes she would allow me to hang out and spend the weekends with her. I remember she had a room decorated in all of this colorful Greek letters. I later find out that the Greek letters represented a sorority. I wanted to be just like my auntie Nicole. She became my role model.

Sadly, my uncle and her divorced, but that did not end our relationship. During my early childhood years, I visited my Auntie

Nicole during the holidays and summer months in her hometown where she had moved back to after the divorce.

She introduced me to the children Bible stories. She would always buy me, Bible storybooks, and workbooks. Nicole even introduced me to the Lord's Prayer. I remember feeling awkward that I had not already known the Lord's Prayer by then, but I was appreciative that she taught it to me.

Throughout the years, we continued to spend time together, and we stayed in contact with one another until I reached college. We still keep in touch from time to time but not nearly as much as we did in the past. As you can predict, Nicole has a special place in my heart because she went beyond the call of duty to be there for me, especially after my uncle and her divorced.

The next set of angels that came into my life is an extraordinary group of women whom I call my "sorors." When I enrolled in college, I had my heart set on joining a sorority just like my Auntie Nicole. I scouted the campus looking for the Greek letter girls that I admired so much as a young child. It should not shock you to discover that by the end of my first year of college, I had not only found the sorority girls, but I had pledged and was officially a member of the organization.

I did not understand how much these women would help mold and shape me. They became like the big sisters I never had. I even gained some little sisters along the way, too. Even though we have had our share of highs and lows, we still manage to remain in contact with each other because we have grown to genuinely love and support one another through the years.

My sorority sisters inspire me in more ways than I can express, and I love them like family. If it had not been for this special group of women, I would not have graduated college. We support and encourage one another even after college graduation, and that demonstrates true sisterhood. Once again, God positioned a group of outstanding women in my life that went beyond the call of duty to help guide my path towards greatness.

The next set of angels God positioned in my life is a special group of friends who have become my family. These are the people who were in the battle with me when my life came crashing down right before my eyes. They were there standing right beside me in the midst of it all. They were also the ones that held me up when I could not stand on my own. They were Kelly, Tasha, Ryan, and Sheila. Yes, these are my four crazy friends.

Yes, I call them crazy because whenever I needed to give the devil a butt-whopping, they would be right there with me, and with their prayer belts wrapped around their waist. They are the people whom I called on when I was at my lowest. When it appeared like I was losing it all—my family, my health, and my life—they would pray for me, and it would bring life to me. They would drag me out of the house to fellowship with them during those times when I wanted to lie in bed and die. They would refer me to books to read and seek out spirit-filled counselors to help lift me up.

My four crazy friends refused to sit back and let me die on their watch. They were my guardian angels that God sent in the form of friends to stand in the gap when I ran out of strength to stand in faith on my own. Yes, God positions people in your life to stand in faith and believe in His promises when you are not strong enough or are too fearful to do so on your own. Praise God! I am so humbled and grateful to have such special people in my corner. They are not only just my friends but they have become my family, and I love them in more ways than I can express. Glory is to God! Who has God positioned in your life to stand in faith, pray and support you when you are down and out?

I met Kelly in the year 2009 while at work. She and I were the school's guidance counselors. I instantly felt comfortable with her, and that is not normal for me. The deep-rooted trust issues I battled typically caused me to withdraw and not share my personal side or have open conversations with people, especially women. I felt so comfortable and safe with her that I instantly just opened up one day and began to share with her things about my personal problems, such as my failing marriage, the abortion I had, and work-related concerns.

Kelly came into my life right before the fall. I was battling a high-risk pregnancy; my marriage was in shambles and our work environment was, to say the least, stressful. Kelly made me feel safe because she listened and she did not pass judgment on me. She offered me good sound advice, and she understood my perspective about things.

We gelled so well that we became sisters. We call each other sister, and for humor, we sometimes sing to one another Shug Avery's song, "Sister," from the movie "The Color Purple." Kelly gave me the appetite and passion for living fruitfully. We would be in each other's office planning activities for our students all while sharing our ideas about our future hopes and dreams. Her jovial and upbeat spirit carried me when I was battling with the spirit of apathy. There were days when I wanted to be at home, in bed and left to die; and then Kelly would call and convince me to coach the girl's track team with her or to go here or there. It was as if God sent her in my life to keep the fire of life burning inside of me on a daily basis.

One day I shared a story that I had begun to write with her. She excitedly verbalized her commentary, and she said something like this, "Giiiirrrlll, you have to finish this book because I did not want to stop reading it." Her reaction helped me to move past my fears of writing. If my sister felt that I was a good enough writer, then I was good enough. "As iron sharpens iron, so one man sharpens another." (Proverbs 27:17.)

One school year, our principal announced that there was a decrease in funding and a guidance counselor position was one of the positions that she had to cut. Kelly and I, the inseparable two, had to learn how to work separately, but that did not end our relationship. After her departure from the school, we continued to communicate and pray together. For in the Bible it reads, "Again, I tell you that if two of you on earth agree about anything you ask for, it will be done for you by my Father in heaven. For where two or three come together in my name, there am I with them." (Mathew 18:19-20.)

Most of our conversations were about God. We talked about our love for our Father, the experiences we have had that has brought us closer to Him, the things we've learned about Him, our dreams, our goals, and our fears. If it had not been for Kelly being there at work with me every day urging and encouraging me, I do not feel that I would have been able to carry on my duties at work as efficiently. God knew exactly who to place in my life to help me when I did not have the strength to hold myself up.

Ryan and Tasha are my married friends. I met Tasha in middle school. She was the first friendly face I encountered at school. I was new at the school. Since I had difficulties opening up and talking to people, the girls perceived me as being stuck-up, or they would say, "She thinks she is all that." Little did they know that "thinking that I was all that" was the farthest thought in my mind. I was thinking about my plans for high school and boys, of course, but I did not think of myself as even pretty.

The childhood trauma I endured caused me to develop shell-shocked symptoms and behavior, and that is why I did not talk to people much. "Shell-shock" is an old mental health diagnosis that some soldiers who were in the war received as a result of witnessing so much death. It caused them to have depression, sleeplessness, anxiety and extreme fear. I did not want my family secrets exposed so I created an image of myself as one who did not have any struggles in life and that I came from a well-to-do family. In reality, that was far from the truth. I could not open up and be transparent with others until after I had been around them for a long enough time to feel comfortable. I remember a time in middle school when some girls harassed me in the cafeteria during lunch. I was sitting conversing with a few boys, and the next thing I knew someone had thrown some food at me. A group of girls sitting at a nearby table was throwing food at me. I did not say anything out of fear and embarrassment. A few people did speak up in my defense and demanded that they stop throwing food at me, which they eventually did but not without making a few snide remarks.

After feeling alone and targeted by a group of "mean girls," Tasha was the person who offered me a genuine smile and said hello to me in passing. She was extremely friendly, and I was not used to females being kind to me. I was more used to them being mean and saying things about me behind my back. Tasha and I did not establish a friendship until high school. We were both in the band, so we spent a great deal of time together. I felt comfortable and safe around her and apparently the feelings were mutual because we clicked and remained friends ever since.

While in college, Tasha met Ryan, and they eventually married. Through my close friendship with Tasha, it was natural for Ryan and me to connect with as friends as well. It was Ryan and Tasha that landed me in the church that opened my eyes to the spiritual side of Christianity. I often shared with them the struggles I dealt with after having an abortion and then becoming a single-parent a year later. They were also my support during the divorce process.

Ryan and Tasha ministered the Word of God to me on those days when I needed it most. I would call them early in the morning or late at night feeling heartbroken and in tears. They would preach, teach and pray with me until I felt better again. They often would pull me out of the house to fellowship with them to avoid me from sinking into a bottomless pit of misery.

One day they told me about a church that they were visiting, and I went with them one Sunday. I answered the altar call for prayer because I was a member of the church that my family attends at that time. A few days later someone from the church called to pray with me. I was genuinely impressed with the follow-up call. I had not experienced a church family that took the time to call and simply pray with me. I was happy to find a church where I felt safe and comfortable attending. The people who served in the ministry who I encountered whenever I would visit there made me feel welcomed. It should not surprise you to know that Ryan, Tasha, and I eventually joined this church.

I met Sheila while in college. She joined the same sorority as me. Sheila also worked at that same school where I worked. However, it was not until we connected at church that we truly became friends. One day I saw her at church, and we have been inseparable since that day. We attended the "Post Encounter" weekend class that the church offers to new members. It is a weekend getaway from the distractions at home, like TV, friends, and your kids, so that you can begin the process of "shedding off the old man" and begin to learn how to live in your spirit man.

I was pregnant with my daughter when I decided to go on the trip. Sheila went too, so we were roommates. I remember feeling a little disappointed because I was married and my spouse did not sign on to journey along this path with me. However, I was determined to learn to live in a manner that was pleasing to God, so I continued the journey without him. Nevertheless, I learned a lot, and Sheila and I grew stronger and closer to God. There were times when I would call or text her and say one single word, "pray." No explanations were required because sometimes that was all I could muster to say. Sheila is not only my soror, but she is my friend, my church family, and she has become my family.

Last but not least, my church family. I did not know many Bible verses, Christian songs, or understand the spiritual messages that are in the Bible until I encountered this Spirit-led church. The bishop of the church teaches his congregation the Word of God like a bible class, by referencing scripture in his teaching. He breaks down the terminology of words by providing us with their definition to broaden our understanding of the Word.

The bishop's approach was more like a father or older brother figure, and the way he delivered God's Word made me want to apply the Word in my life. He does not cast judgment on you or make you feel guilty because of how he relates to his congregation. He encourages and inspires us to live according to the Word by allowing the Holy Spirit to guide your path. The bishop also understands the growth process with new Christians, and he often shares personal stories and struggles that he overcame, and this helped me see the

Lord working through him. I felt welcomed and safe at the church. I did not only see God working through the bishop but in all the other church leaders and helpers too.

My first visit to the church was in 2003. I made the decision to join it in the summer of 2008 because I had finally found a pastor and church family where I could clearly see and feel the anointing of God operating in the house of the Lord. I believe that my bishop genuinely loves the people in the church, and he delivers messages from the heart. This revelation inspired me because all the while I had been searching for a church family where I could rest in God's Word and learn the truth without all of the religious traditions overshadowing things.

In 2008 during one of my visits, I answered the altar call, and I joined the church. Yes, it took me five long years before I finally joined the church. I had not become a member earlier because I was a member of another church. However, honestly, I was more of a visitor to my former church because my attendance was comparable to a truant high school student on the verge of dropping out of school.

Although I was not committing awful or evil acts, I was in the world practicing sin like fornication and drinking; and to me, that was bad enough. I was still spiritually dead. Before joining the church, I had no background knowledge about the spiritual gifts Jesus talked about in John 14. I was blind, so I could only understand scripture in my physical ability and natural mind. I always sensed that there was something higher than myself that lived deep within me, and I now know that God's presence was with me my whole life.

While in the new members' class, one of the ministers began to teach us about praying in tongues. Now, I heard about those so-called, "crazy religious folks" who spoke in tongues but I never encountered anyone who prayed in tongues, or, at least, I never saw or heard them. I just remember overhearing someone else talking about people who prayed in tongues, and the message I received from listening to him was to stay away from those "crazy tongue praying folks." The devil does sly things to keep you away from the truth. The memory of that conversation I heard came to my mind when we discussed it in the membership class.

However, when the ministers referenced scripture in their teaching of it I instantly believed and accepted it. I began praying in the Holy Spirit that same day because I made a decision to believe. In Romans 8:26-27 Paul, an apostle, and servant of God, gives Saints insight about praying in the spirit, "In the same way, the Spirit helps us in our weakness. We do not know what we ought to pray for, but the Spirit himself intercedes for us with groans that words cannot express. And He who searches our hearts knows the mind of the Spirit because the Spirit intercedes for the saints by God's will." I was sold when I discovered this truth because I felt that I had a hidden prayer box deep within me that was about to explode. Quite naturally, I began praying in the Spirit, and I felt relieved.

Before joining the church, I had a strong desire to learn the Word of God by scripture. I wanted to understand the mysteries deep within the Bible, so God sent me to this church to gain wisdom and understanding of the gift of the Holy Spirit that God gives to His children, the believers. Since the summer of 2008 when I answered the altar call, I had been growing in the spirit; however, it was not until 2010 that I began to read and meditate on John 14.

Chapter Eight

Spiritual Boot Camp: Jesus is your master teacher

"I have been crucified with Christ, and I no longer

live, but Christ lives in me." (Galatians 2:20)

I encountered a woman who lives in the spirit of God, and she told me that the Lord wanted me to read John 14. She also said that the Spirit of the Lord instructed her to tell me to read Mark 5:24-34. It is the scripture about Jesus healing the woman with the blood issue. At the time, I was going through a divorce, so I knew I was in a spiritual war zone. When two people, man, and woman, commit before God to join as one, and if they divorce it is like tearing their spirits apart. Trust me, it hurts.

The enemy comes in with his thunderous roaring, and it can cause immature Christians and nonbelievers to succumb to his evil torments. During the divorce process and for some time afterward, the devil began to attack me ferociously. I was in the twilight zone with these weird activities swirling within and all around me that I understood, yet I could not verbalize to anyone else; nor could I explain to my ex what the enemy was doing to us in a way that he could receive it because I was still so spiritually immature.

My carnal man took over, and I tried to fight the battle myself, but that left me feeling like a fool. Oooohhh, that devil thought he had me going, and he did have my mind at times; but unbeknownst to me, God's protective hand was in the midst.

When you grow in the spirit, you begin to identify with the people in the Bible. I felt like Jesus because of all of the adversities that I endured. Like Him, I was mocked, ridiculed, tried, beaten, spit on, and stabbed in the back by others. One of Jesus' disciples, Judas Iscariot, betrayed Him. He set Jesus up and handed Him over to the multitude of people with clubs and swords that the high priests and elders sent to capture Him. Another disciple, Peter, denied that he knew Jesus three times even after Jesus told him that he would do that.

I imagined that the multitude of people who were sent to arrest Jesus made condescending comments like, "Why haven't you saved yourself since you say that you are the Son of God?" The devil creates thoughts that attempt to make you believe that God is not in the midst of our troubles. What appeared to be Jesus' worst night became the best night for all of us. Jesus defeated the enemy, saved us from our sin, and He lives! As for the disciple Judas, after realizing his deception he killed himself, and the other one, Peter, went out and remorsefully cried when he remembered what Jesus said to him about disowning Him three times by the time the rooster crowed (see Mathew 2:5 & 26:75).

When it appeared like God was not present, and everything in my life was falling apart I kept my heart and mind fixed on the Lord. I prayed in tongues so much because I did not know what to pray for using words. I had run out of words to say, and the only words I had left inside of me were groans. My spirit was crying and pleading for the Lord to show up in my life quick to deliver me from the hurt and pain.

In my suffering, I did not give up the hope that Jesus Christ would save me from my present trials of life. In Romans 8:18, "I consider that our present sufferings are not worth comparing with the glory that will be revealed in us." I encountered the spirit-filled woman several times during this ordeal, and she told me to read Psalms 34, 35, 36, 37, 70, 91, and 127. She told me to read Psalm 34, always. I read those Psalms, and I continue to do so today, especially Psalm 34 and 91. "I will extol the Lord at all times; his praise will always be on my lips." (Psalm 34:1.) "For he will command his angels concerning you to guard you in all your ways; they will lift you up in their hands so that you will not strike your foot against a stone." (Psalm 91:11-12.) I carried those Psalms in my heart because I knew that for me to live through the drama, I had to hold on to the Lord's unchanging hand.

By the end of 2010, I was divorced and sick. I felt defeated, but I kept believing and asking God to do for me what David prayed in Psalm 70:1, "Hasten, O God, to save me; oh God come quickly to help me." I kept my focus on God even in those moments when it appeared as if I was losing the battle. I was mocked, ridiculed, and beaten, too. I heard the enemy say things like "Sister Campbell, stop praying in that crazy tongue. Where is your God at now? You better get your anointing oil."

Isn't it funny how the devil tries to fool you by tricking you into thinking that you are worthless, unloved and that Jesus does not have the power to truly heal, yet alone save you? Whoever is reading this, I pray that your eyes are being pried open and that your ears are unplugged so that you can see and hear the Word of God. Do not be tricked by the devil's evil ploys or give in to his trickery. His schemes set the stage for you to do something to yourself or someone else that goes against God's Word. The devil is a liar from the pit of Hades, and that is where he will remain; right under my feet! For it is written, "You will tread upon the lion and cobra; you will trample the great lion and the serpent." (Psalm 91:13.)

Early in the year 2012, I kept receiving two messages from random people, "God wants to heal you," and "You are going to live for a long time." A few of these people I did not even know, yet they felt compelled to deliver the message to me. I remember becoming frustrated with God after hearing someone tell me that He wanted to heal me. I thought to myself, "God, what is stopping you from healing me because I am tired of feeling pain and sickness in my body."

Since July 3, 2012, God has removed the veil from over my eyes, and I have gained wisdom and understanding. I now realize that when God heals, he heals you from all the internal poison within the crevices of your soul. For some people God will heal you right there on the spot and your symptoms will miraculously disappear. For others, they must get their healing by first removing the internal emotional wounds before the physical wounds can begin to heal. The sad part is that some people think that because they do not have an illness they do not need healing. We all come to the table with something. For some of us, it is diabetes, for others it is cancer, and some of us are perfectly healthy, or so we think.

We are all predisposed to have some form of a medical condition based on our family history. Doctors are aware of this fact, which is why they ask about common illnesses that your family members may have had, such as high blood pressure or hypertension, diabetes, or cancer. The trend is that if someone in your family has a medical condition, then you are likely to develop that same sickness or disease as you grow older. Of course, you can avoid developing certain medical conditions with proper diet and exercise, but it goes even deeper than that.

It is imperative that you accept Jesus into your heart and allow Him to heal you from deeply hidden emotional wounds before stress from living in this world causes you to develop a sickness or disease that will eventually, if not managed properly, cause you to give in and die. This process is required to wipe out all traces of family curses from your life. Family curses can range from mental health or physical health issues, sexual perversion, or anger issues. Many of you do not think you need healing unless they have some form of medical diagnosis from a doctor, whether it is for mental health or a physical health issue. Therefore, you do not think that anything is affecting you.

The problem with that thought process is that you must renew your mind daily to defeat the enemy of the world (see Romans 12:2). The way this world is set up, it puts things in the atmosphere to taint your spirit on a daily basis. It is imperative that you guard the things you see, hear, feel, and taste because there are things that may trigger you to have negative thoughts or perform an action that could create some form of unpleasant result.

There is an evil spirit named "pride" that hinders many of us from letting go of old hurts, and because of this, you have difficulty accepting or believing in Jesus. I have heard statements such as this one: "If Jesus is real, then he would cure me of this or he would not have allowed the catastrophe to happen." Well, the secret cause of many adverse events or results is because of you. Your thoughts, actions, and words play a significant role in creating whatever event occurs, whether good or bad. You are your worst enemy, and pride is one of the things that make you so. Yes, God placed us all here for a particular purpose. We are here for His pleasure, and because we are His children we get to reap the fruit of the spirit, but only if we are obedient and follow the example of righteous living through His Son, Jesus. He cannot have a prideful and egotistical spirit working for Him.

Let us look at Satan as an example of how pride can cause God to remove your name from the Book of Life and keep you from entering Heaven. Satan was an angel, and God favored him. God made him highest of all the angels; therefore, he had special privileges. Then Satan became big headed and arrogant by thinking that he could become God. When his pride took over, he tried to be God and not a servant of God. It was then that God threw him out of the Kingdom (see Ezekiel 28:12-19 and Isaiah 14:12-15).

For some people, God heals right on the spot and for others, the healing occurs gradually. Even children who lived in a spirit-filled home know that they need Jesus to live in the fruit of the Spirit as adults. "The fruit of the Spirit is love, joy, peace, patience, kindness, goodness, faithfulness, gentleness, and self-control." (Galatians 5:22-23.) People who live by the Holy Spirit know how to flow through their problems efficiently, live peaceably and be happy, loving and healthy because they follow the ways of the Lord. Proverbs 22:6 reads, "Train a child in the way he should go, and when he is old he will not turn from it."

You may be thinking that I grew up in the church, and I know the Word because I can quote scripture. That is all good, but if you have not been born of water and spirit, then you will not enter God's Holy Kingdom (see John 3:5-7). Proper instruction and training include how to live a good lifestyle by following biblical teachings, as well as how to live in the Holy Spirit. If you have not received proper instruction on how to live in the Spirit, you have backslidden, or you simply just do not believe—then line up to receive your healing, please!

Even the most mature Christians understand that "we all have sinned and fallen short of the glory of God." However, it is our faith in Jesus that frees us from the punishment of our sins. Our Father in Heaven has restored us through the atonement of His Son, Jesus (see Romans 3:23-24). If you are not living out God's purpose for your life and are not operating in the Holy Spirit, then it is imperative that you link up with Jesus so that He can heal you and retrain your mind. Every day I make it a habit of operating in God's purpose for my life and allow the gift of the Holy Spirit to guide me. I may not get it right all of the time, but like Paul states in Philippians 3:14, "I press on toward the goal to win the prize for which God has called me heavenward in Christ Jesus."

If you look at my history, I endured many challenges, and I learned some valuable life-lessons. One of the most important lessons I learned is that the only way to the Father is through Jesus. I tried living life my way for so long, and my way always landed me in some trouble. Jesus said in Matthew 7:24, "Therefore, everyone who hears these words and puts them into practice is like a wise man who built his house on the rock."

I am a living witness that my life did not transform for the better until I understood the sacrifice Jesus made to save me. I was a believer in God, but I did not fully comprehend Jesus' purpose out of ignorance. I believed that Jesus died to save me from my sins. However, I did not understand the magnitude of the sacrifice that He made for us until I touched his cloak and activated my faith in Him, as the woman with the issue of the blood did that day she encountered Jesus (see Mark 5:25-34).

Then Jesus showed up, and he healed me from all the emotional baggage that caused the stress that in turn caused the RA and dermatomyositis symptoms to form in my body. Now, when I get symptoms of RA flares up, I stop and assess my thoughts, actions, and words. Usually, when symptoms show up in my body, I discover that I allowed the enemy to enter my spirit, creating stress, worry or anxiety to manifest in my thoughts. I make it a practice not to go to bed without renewing my mind and refocusing my thoughts back on Jesus on a daily basis.

When I had let go of myself and allowed Jesus, who is Lord, to take control of my life, instantly He revealed my purpose for being here and I began my healing process. Within a four-month timeframe, God showed me so much about myself, as well as given me wisdom and understanding of Scripture. Every day, I am more humbled and obedient than I was before. I am always learning and growing by allowing the Holy Spirit to guide me.

When the Lord uncovers your eyes, you can read the Bible with new understanding, and you can hear God speak to you. Then you will see how much of an adulterer or adulteress you were to God when you were out committing sins and turning your back on Him— the one that created you and loves you unconditionally. It is then that you become humbled and can sincerely offer Him repentance.

The Holy Spirit guided me to read the book of Jeremiah. When I read it, I could hear God speaking to me. I could clearly hear the voice of the Lord and what I heard made me feel so unworthy of his love and mercy. I felt ashamed of my sinful actions so much that I truly repented and changed my ways. I felt so sorry for all of those countless times that I turned away from Jesus to follow man. My pride began to evaporate into thin air, and I start to feel so grateful to have God's favor in my life.

As I read the book of Jeremiah, I heard a parent who was struggling with trying to understand why His children turned their backs on Him. His children were committing all types of horrible sins. I kept hearing God's voice pleading to us saying, "If you change your ways and turn back to me, then I will bless you, and you will glorify me" (see Jeremiah). Our Father wants what is best for us just as parents want the best for their children. Parents continuously forgive and give their children numerous chances to correct their errors. That is the same type of love that God has for all of us regardless of how terrible the deed or act. He will still accept you if you sincerely change your ways and accept His Son, Jesus, into your heart. When I heard God speak to me through Jeremiah, I realized just how much He loves me, and I felt so honored, yet I felt little and undeserving because of my disobedience.

Through my healing process, the Lord revealed to me how I developed rheumatoid arthritis. The mistakes I made in my relationship with my dad, the men who I allowed to misuse His temple, as well as my prideful and other sinful behaviors caused me so much stress that it opened the door for RA to enter and run havoc in my body. When you allow Jesus to heal you, He takes you through a process that I have termed "spiritual boot camp." Yes, the process is tough, and you have to be fully equipped to endure it because it breaks you down. The breaking-down process humbles and develops your character.

The first phase of the process requires you to look at yourself in the mirror. It is imperative to look at yourself first so that you can identify the ungodly characteristics within you. It is tough to acknowledge the errors of your ways, especially when it seems so much easier to blame fault on someone else for your problems.

Be careful with easy fixes because that is how the enemy sneaks in and wreaks havoc in your life. Take a person who has a high-stress job. He resorts to taking prescription medication to cope with the stress. Next, he has formed a habit and an addiction.

Here is another demonstration of how the enemy keeps the vision of yourself blurred, causing you to wreak havoc on yourself. Take a young girl abused sexually by her uncle. She blamed her parents because she believed they were the ones who allowed him to stay in their home and molest her. She grew up resenting her parents for not realizing what her uncle did to her when they allowed him to live there because she felt that they should have known something was wrong. She gave them clues when she started acting out in school, getting bad grades, and running away from home. She had emotional hurts far beyond her control, and as a result, even in her adulthood, she consistently found herself in bad situations. She always placed the reason for making her bad decisions on someone else. She thought that it was not her fault because she did not have a choice, just as she did not have a choice when it came to her uncle staying in her parent's home and molesting her at night.

Even I used to blame my dad for some of my issues, but at the end of the day, I had the free will to choose the decisions I made, whether they were right, wrong, good, bad or indifferent. No one forced me to make those choices. I made them of my free will. The way I chose to handle my problems, the men I selected to date, as well as the places I socialized at were all my choices.

It is hard to accept that you are the cause of most of your problems because it exposes the evil nature that can exist within you. At some point, you cannot keep blaming others for your errors. You must grow up and accept the choices you made and your reasons for making them. When I looked at myself and realized that I was the source of a lot of my problems, I crumbled because I saw how selfish, prideful, and self-centered I had become. I also saw the shameful behaviors I acted out, such as being promiscuous, rude, and unforgiving. In Mark 7:20-23, Jesus said, "What comes out of a man is what makes him unclean. For from within, out of men's hearts, come evil thoughts, sexual immorality, theft, murder, adultery, greed, malice, deceit, lewdness, envy, slander, arrogance, and folly. All these evils come from inside and make a man unclean." It was a challenge to look at myself and not place the blame for my bad choices on someone else because I had to admit that my impure thoughts led me to make some awful decisions that caused me to harm others and myself. If it had not been for Jesus, I would still be on this self-destructive cycle until I eventually died due to suicide.

Many more people commit suicide than the reported statistical data suggests. Suicide is not just hanging yourself in the basement or placing a gun to your head and pulling the trigger. It is also the result of playing Russian roulette with your life, period. Any form of self-destructive behavior that leads to death, I consider being a suicide.

For instance, continuously overeating to the point where you are diagnosed with a medical condition is a sin, and if you continue to eat foods that are not healthy for your body, it will cause you to die. Gluttony is an example of suicide because you are consistently placing unhealthy amounts of food that your body can no longer tolerate inside of it.

Underlying issues or problems that are not visible cause people to make unhealthy and unwise decisions. The reason someone may act self-destructively comes from things that he or she may have been exposed to as a child or even in the womb. If you take a close look at your family history and childhood, you can begin to identify family curses and events that may have traumatized you.

Early childhood trauma causes deep emotional scars, which can cause those who experienced the trauma to cope with problems ineffectively. It can potentially lead them to self-harm such as cutting, abuse drugs or alcohol or commit suicide. Their inability to deal with their emotions and stress-related situations can also cause them to hurt other people. Often, when you see or hear that someone has "snapped" or committed a horrific crime it usually stems from a trauma that occurred early in their life. The cycle of stressful situations arising from negative thoughts and hurt emotions literally took them over the edge causing them to act in a destructive manner. The last straw or that final stressful episode was the spark that ignited the gas, which caused the person to explode or snap.

There is a television show called Snapped that shows women who kill themselves because of a romantic love that went wrong, due to abuse, greed, obsession or some other form of cruel intention. If you were to take a walk down "memory lane" and have them share information about their childhood, you would see how and when the enemy entered their mind causing them to make the deadly decision to kill or hurt themselves and others.

The devil cannot do anything to you. He only sets up the stage for you to commit horrible acts to yourself and others. God has already restored us and offers a way out of the devil's hands, and that is through Jesus. John 10:10 reads, "The thief comes only to steal and kill and destroy; I have come that they may have life and have it to the full."

Family curses, such as mental health disorders or health conditions that generations of family members are diagnosed with can be destroyed when the culprit is identified and called out. An example of a family curse is someone with a family history of mental health disorder, such as schizophrenia. When Jesus was in the synagogue teaching he recognized that a man there was possessed by an evil spirit, so He called the evil spirit out of the man, and it came out of him (see Mark 1:23-26).

Have you noticed that many family secrets stem from a sinful act or event that the family does not want to expose? Instead of talking about the issue and seeking help so that the family can receive healing, they choose to keep quiet and shun those who try to speak about it. Family secrets are the devil's scheme to keep the curse flowing from generation to generation.

Here is another example of a generational curse: a family formed out of incest. The uncle married his niece, and they had a male child. Their son got married, and he had a son. The grandson battled with acts of sexually perverted behavior that eventually landed him in prison. The family was puzzled because they did not understand why he would commit such horrible acts. It was not until the evil spirit was identified, the incest, and it was called out in the name of Jesus, did the detrimental effects from it begin to flee from the family and the curse was removed. The family could then forgive, heal, love and move on with their lives in peace.

Chapter Nine

The Unveiling: Gaining Wisdom and Understanding

"By wisdom a house is built, and through understanding it is established; through knowledge its rooms are filled with rare and beautiful treasures." —Proverbs 24:3-4

As I mentioned before, when I experience symptoms of an RA flare-up, I stop to think what may have triggered it or what happened to cause the flare to occur. Stress resulting from my early childhood trauma and other dramatic experiences throughout my adulthood, as well as how I dealt with problems that happened in my life, are the underlying culprits that caused me to develop this condition. Every day I practice releasing my cares over to the Lord more regularly. It states in the Bible to "cast your cares on the Lord, and he will sustain you; He will never let the righteous fall" (Psalm 55:22).

Usually, when I am stressed or anxious, it is due to worrying about a situation that is beyond my control. Did you know that worrying is a sin? When you worry, it means that you are not standing in faith. When you do not have faith in God to know that everything will work out in your favor regardless of what the outcome looks like it limits what God can do for you. Jesus commands us not to worry. In Matthew 6:25-34, Jesus says, "Therefore I tell you, do not worry about your life, what you will eat or drink; or about your body; what you will wear; do not worry about tomorrow...." Jesus says if He takes care of the birds in the air then surely God will take care of you.

I know that it is difficult not to worry when your bank account is in the negative, and the rent is due. I have learned that when I release my cares over to God, He supplies all of my needs. I was in situations when I did not have the funds to pay a bill. However, when I cast my care over to the Lord, He miraculously provided the means for me to pay the bill. The more I let go and let God control my life, the fewer symptoms of stress and worry I have.

I am the type of a person who hauls many cares around. I even carry you in my heart, which is why I am writing this book. It took a lot of time, energy, and countless internal battles with fear and doubt throughout the writing process to produce this story. Yes, there were days when I dealt with flare-ups writing this book, but I refused to let the devil defeat me by keeping me in silence. I was not going to allow my insecurities stop me from doing what God called me to do. I noticed that after each chapter I wrote, I felt more relieved and less stressed. God came and healed me from all of that emotional baggage I had been carrying throughout the years. Now, I am unloading one care at a time.

I understand the Lord's great purpose and just how much our Father God loves us; I give myself to Him every day. I may not get it right all of the time but every day I strive to live His will for my life. A fire is burning inside of me and the flame ignited in me is God. I will no longer water-down the God that resides in me. Jesus is Lord! He is the one who healed me, not a doctor or a prescription. I value doctors, nurses, and medical science because the Lord purposefully created them to help sustain us when we are battling sickness, pain, or disease.

Another trigger that sparks symptoms of a flare-up is inadequate rest. When my body felt worn and tired the joints in my hands, knees and arms become inflamed, and it can be very painful to walk and lift objects. Putting on my clothes as well as opening containers is very challenging at times. I often feel feverish and weak during flare-ups. I use to be the type of person who could constantly move about, and I operated in a very fast-paced state of mind. Now I have to slow my pace and incorporate rest periods in my day so that I do not overwhelm myself. I often reflect on Matthew 11:28-30 when

Jesus says, "Come to me, all you who are weary and burdened, and I will give you rest. Take my yoke upon you and learn from me, for I am gentle and humble in heart, and you will find rest for your souls. For my yoke is easy and my burden is light."

I am a living witness to the fact that since I began to learn and live in the way of Jesus, I have found peaceful rest and my load is lightening. My mind is free from all of the clutter that clouded my vision, purpose and true identity from forming. Now, my thoughts are on following God's way of living in love, peace and joy, and less on the cares of the world. The healing of my body manifests itself the more I follow and implement Jesus' way of life in my daily lifestyle.

Some people give up on believing in Jesus' healing or just do not believe that is why they have not received their healing. Others receive temporary healing only to discover that the disease or condition has come back, and then their hope is shattered. As a witness of Jesus' healing, I can truthfully reveal to you that it does not matter what the medical reports say; you know that Jesus has healed you because of your changed mind, heart and lifestyle. The cares of this world slowly vanish away. The doubts and fears that crippled you from becoming dissipate and a new person is formed. When you allow His Holy Spirit to guide you then with ease, you can move past the barriers that the devil sets up to distract you or throw you off course. You will find that when troubles come you flow through them more efficiently, and they do not keep you down.

As for me, I noticed that when troubles come my way I do not dwell on the problem for months or years as I had in the past. Now, it is becoming easier for me to forgive and let go so that I can continue to operate in love. I no longer shun those who offend me in some way. However, if I need to place distance in the relationship so that I do not fall for the enemy's tricks to get me to cross over into sin, then I will do so, and will continue to pray for the person with a sincere heart. When Jesus heals you, he heals your mind, heart, body and soul. You truly become a transformed and new person.

Before sharing my story, I struggled internally with fears and negative thoughts because I was still holding onto the world. I did not have enough faith in the promises of God to believe that I could have or become anything more than what I already had become. I settled for less than God's best, and I was unhappy and unfulfilled in life up until the time I accepted Jesus. When I touched Jesus' cloak and stood in faith He showed up and just like that; I was healed. The healing process was not easy because, as I mentioned earlier, it required me to face my demons. In order for me to look at myself in the mirror and travel back in time to my early childhood, I had to lay down my pride, fears, resentment, hate, and insecurities and rely on God completely.

Relying solely on God was difficult because I had relied on myself for so long that it was hard for me to let go and allow God to take control of my life. I still struggle with submitting my will over to Him at times, but every day I try to give more of myself to Him than I did the day before. No, I do not feel as if I am an expert yet in scripture. I still struggle with quoting scriptures verbatim, and I still refer to the table of contents to locate books in the Bible; however, one thing that I am sure of is my changed life. The more I enmesh myself in the daily reading of scripture and Christian books and going to church to hear the Word of God, the more I grow in the Spirit. I also grow and learn more about God when I hear people's victory stories.

Victory stories are stories about people who rose above adversity and succeeded. Some of the victory stories that I heard about were not written in a book. These stories came from the mouths of people who experienced a trial and shared their testimony with me. I can only imagine how many books there would be that showcased and glorified God if only those of us who are living witness to His grace and mercy would write it down on a scroll. Think about how many movies, stage plays, and music would show up to honor our God. The enemy would surely get trampled on because the primary influencing arena, the media, would have more and more Godly stories to share and less of that filth that is spreading all over the big screen, television, and radio stations to taint our mind and spirit.

You know God created us with the ability to conquer our enemies. We are well equipped for the battle because all we need is love. God commanded us to love one another just as He loves us (see John 15:9-17). Love conquers all. It holds the power to erase all evilness from our hearts and minds. Love is a powerful tool if only we learn how to use it the way God intends for us.

The devil has absolutely no power over us. The only power he has is the power that we give him. We give our power away the more we allow him to take control of our mind. When our thoughts grow cold with malice, jealousy, resentment, and hatred, then we open the door for Satan to come in with his legions of bad friends to move us further away from operating in love. Instead, we begin to act in lust, pride, fear, doubt, insecurity, hate and greed. It is these negative thoughts that lead you astray. We are making music, movies, books, and living our lives continuously out of alignment with the way of life that Jesus modeled for us.

Nowadays, it is easier to do wrong and engage in sin than it is to do the right thing. I bet you that I can find more people to follow me in doing something wrong than I can find to support me to do something right. For instance, I can quickly find someone who will be willing to engage in perverted sex, gossip, fighting, etc., with me than I can find someone who is willing to follow God's way of living with me, like attending church with me on a regular basis. It is a challenge to go against the grain by doing what is right because we live in a world that is, to state it simply, wrong. It's easier to turn the other cheek and sweep errors under the rug than it is to stand up and call out our evilness or bad behavior because of fear. Fear of looking like the troublemaker when you are the one who is trying to implement biblical standards is an example of backward thinking. The devil has this world and our minds spinning in circles, and if we continue to operate in his worldly system then, as Psalm 34:21 says, "Evil will slay the wicked." This means your evil ways and desires will eventually kill you.

My brothers and sisters, it is time you obtain wisdom and understanding so that you get off the devil's "wheel of life" and connect with Jesus so that you can form in His image and likeness. God sent Jesus here so that He could coach and train us on how to live a righteous life so that we can enjoy the fruits of life. Just as with Moses, God tried to give the Israelites laws to follow which He instructed Moses to share. Moses accomplished the noble task of Exodus. God gave signs and wonders to cease the Israelites complaints and to stop them from giving His servant such a hard time. Well, that did not prevent His children from sinning and worshipping idols, so He sent the ultimate redeemer, Jesus Christ, to model and show us the way to our Father God.

Now, we are giving Jesus a hard time by not following His example and seeking God through Him. The devil has set up all of these different religions and false prophets to keep us in darkness and away from the light. I am here to tell you as a living witness that Jesus is the only way to the Father. I, like Paul, had an encounter with our Lord, and He sent people to place salve on my eyes to restore my sight so that He could fill me up with the His Holy Spirit. In my ignorance, I was persecuting Jesus when I chose to follow the ways of the world by my continuous acting and living in my sinful nature, just like Paul did (see Acts 9:3-18).

After you receive healing and restoration, you must go out and share the Good News with others who are blind and trapped in the devil's sticky web of destruction. If a witness of the living God does not help his fellow brother or sister by sharing His evidence and knowledge about Jesus, God will hold you accountable for your brother's sin (see Leviticus 5:1). I had to share my story with you so that I do not continue in sin by not leading you to the living water to receive your salvation. I understand that if you decide not to drink from the living spring water that it is entirely your choice. God has placed an urging inside of me to go out into the darkness and shine His light in your direction to help you. If you reject my help, you are not rejecting me but my Father. The more I resisted His call and chose to follow the wicked and evil ploys that tainted my mind and heart, the more I suffered.

If you continue not to live in love and choose to live in the dark shadows of death, the more corrupt this world will become and you will eventually die. Some of you are already dead spiritually, just like I was. When a person is spiritually dead, he is like a walking zombie going in any direction that the world decides that he should go in. It was not until my old self died and I was reborn again that the world, as well as my life, began to make sense. Before then, I was merely existing and blending in with my surroundings, waiting for my next negative reaction to pay me back for the negative thoughts and actions that I put out in the atmosphere.

No, I did not appear to be a self-destructive ticking time bomb on the exterior, but my interior was battling good and evil thoughts and actions continuously in a rhythmic, circular pattern. You cannot look at me and judge my character by my past transgressions, nor can I judge you for your past offenses. We all fall short of the glory of God sometimes, which is why He instructs us to judge not each other.

What I have discovered is that God does not punish us for our sins, we punish ourselves for the sins we put out in the world. Mistakes are not God's fault, but they are our own; however, our mistakes and misdeeds help us to learn and grow, as opposed to being kept in defeat. Our mistakes and challenges in life are designed to help us mature and to build our character, not to make us feel like wounded animals. When you find yourself making the same mistakes over and over again, then it means that you did not fully understand the error and little or no growth occurred, so you will continuously stay in the same circular pattern until you wise up and get off the wheel.

Every trial or test is set up for your gain so when trouble comes you should rejoice and boastfully glorify God. Roman 5:3, leaves us with this instruction, "Not only so, but we also rejoice in our sufferings because we know that suffering produces perseverance." If you are not careful, you will miss it, and your life will go through continuous destructive patterns that create poverty, strife and misfortune until you come to the realization of life's boomerang effect.

The more you resist and turn against God's way, the more the devil continues to turn you on the wheel towards Hades. A majority of us learned The Golden Rule: "Do unto others as you would have them do unto you." It is a universal law. It crosses religions, traditions, and values. Essentially, what you act upon or think about, whether good or bad, will eventually come back to you. Simply stated, positive thoughts and actions reap positive rewards, and negative thoughts and actions bring forth negative consequences, which ultimately leads to spiritual turmoil.

The only way to retrain your mind and remove your negative way of thinking is to seek Jesus' healing and guidance. Some of you may have heard the cliché "mind over matter." It is more than just a saying. It is a true statement! In 1 Peter 1:23, Peter gives us this instruction, "...prepare your minds for action; be self-controlled; set your hope fully on the grace to be given to you when Jesus Christ is revealed." If you can train your mind to think beyond the present problem, then you will defeat the tricks that the enemy uses to keep your mind in the dark with clutter and confusion, halting you from reaching your full potential.

For instance, if you have pain in your body the only way to retrain your mind so that you can place your focus past the pain and have faith in becoming pain-free is through Jesus. You can attempt to do it alone without Jesus, and you may have temporary success. The devil is a false prophet, and he is a master at manipulating the worldly system to keep you in the dark and away from fully accepting the light which comes from the Word of God. For it is written, in 2 Corinthians 4:4, "The god of this age has blinded the minds of unbelievers so that they cannot see the light of the gospel of the glory of Christ, who is the image of God."

God created us with the ability to defeat our enemies. Who are these enemies? They are the enemies within our minds that come from our heart—doubt, fear, envy, jealousy, murder, sexual perversion, idolatry, lies, worry, anxiety, depression, sickness, and the list goes on. An unclean heart produces evil thoughts that will eventually lead to sin and death if you do not repent and renew your mind. Jesus gave us the commandment to love because if you operate with a heart that is under the authority of love, your thoughts will be clean and pure. God can only grow His fruit in you when you are operating in love. It is important that you remain constant in reading and learning scriptures to keep your heart and mind focused on Jesus.

Jesus is the one who strengthens you in your weakness. The more you lift Jesus' weights, the stronger you become! I do not know about you, but my goal is to get as strong as God allows me to become so that I can secure my spot in Heaven. The corrupt and evil world in which we live in is enough Hades-experience for me not to want to spend the rest of eternity in Satan's home. As I am sharing this story, I can humbly admit that I have not yet arrived, but like Paul, I will "beat my body and make it my slave so that after I have preached to others, I myself will not be disqualified for the prize" (1 Corinthians 27).

When God began to reveal my purpose to me, I did not fully understand it right away. It took some time and effort on my part to gain an understanding of what He was relaying to me. Next, I had to develop my courage muscels and activate my faith in His word to begin the process of operating in my purpose. God urged me to write, and I battled with Him, mostly because of my insecurity—my pride and fears. No one was stopping me from being healed and moving toward my sacred place in the kingdom, but myself. Just like many of you who are reading this book are not operating in your divine purpose. The reason is that you have not fully accepted Jesus because of pride and doubt, and for some because you do not believe that Jesus is the Son of God. It could also be because you do not think that God will provide what He promises to give His children.

I am here to encourage you to stop limiting yourself from reaching your full potential. If you accept Jesus into your heart and believe that He died to save you from your sins, then you are on your way. It is time to activate your faith in Him and follow His lead. The Holy Spirit will guide and instruct you along the way, so you are not alone. Additionally, I advise you to join a spirit-filled church to help you, because you cannot do this alone.

God placed us in this world to love and serve one another. He created us with unique and special gifts to help build up one another. Instead, I see so many of us tearing each other down by acting out the evil intentions that tempt our hearts and minds. Yes, we have temptations, but it does not mean that we should habitually give in to them. I recommend that you join a church and develop relationships with other believers so that when you are weak you can seek others for support.

When I accepted Jesus as my Lord and Savior, I was not attending church regularly. To be honest, I had not been to church for many months until the time that I allowed Him to take control over my life. The Holy Spirit within me instructed me to go back to church and to go back to counseling. When I was going through a divorce and its aftermath, I went to counseling at my church. I stopped attending counseling because I felt I could handle it myself. Well, that was my pride that sprung up because of the insecurities I had, and I was what you called "church hurt." I felt that I needed more help from the church. I wanted the ministers there to be more accessible to me during my time of grief, but what I failed to do was vocalize my needs in a way that could have gotten me the support that I felt I needed. I did not vocalize my needs out of fear and shame. In all honesty, I wanted them to know my issues without me having to tell them everything. I passively retreated inside and decided to handle my problems on my own. Luckily, I had friends and family who were believers, and they were able to keep me encouraged and support me during my time away from the church. The devil sets people up to think they do not need a church family or a community of believers to grow in the spirit. It is an absolute lie from the pit of Hades.

You are a part of the body of Christ, and if a body part is missing then the church cannot function at is optimal best. I feel that this is the reason churches are hurting because the believers are walking away or being nothing more than benchwarmers. I was a bench warmer, too, for years before I decided to begin the process to serve others. I had to resume counseling to help me overcome some lingering issues that still had not resolved. God wanted me healed from the emotional baggage that I was carrying before I could serve Him.

One of the reasons why He created us is to carry out His will and plan. To do His will, you must purge all of the junk that the world has placed inside you to taint and tarnish His most magnificent creation, which is you. God wants us to serve one another with love. He also requires that we honor and glorify His Son Jesus whose spirit lives within each of us. He created each of us with unique gifts to share with one another and build each other up so that we all can enter and enjoy His kingdom.

The gifts and talents that He gave you are to make you prosper and grow. God does not want you to give in to the things of this world that are set up for you to fall victim to defeat, such as financial debt, sickness, heartache, and pain. He has given you power and authority to trample over your enemies, so now it is time to allow Jesus to heal you and begin the process of renewing your mind. Keep the devil where he belongs—right under your feet!

Here is a strategy that I use to battle the enemy. In my mind, I visualize myself slamming the devil and his evil tyrants to the ground and walking on them. I operate under God's authority, and I follow the guidance of the Holy Spirit to instruct my daily path so I will not fail, and you will not either if you just hold on to the Lord's unchanging hand.

God knew that I would not be able to serve in the ministry at my local church due to my past sins until after I proved that I could sustain myself long enough to pass the test of not giving in to my past sinful behavior, such as drinking and fornication. He instructed me to write this book and share my spiritual growth and to teach others. God knew I had a burning desire in my heart to serve Him and others, and if I had lingered there in my desire and not operate in the area that I was passionate about, then the enemy would have come in with his evil friends to attack me.

The urging was so intense that I could no longer ignore it as I had in the past, so I found a website designer to create a website for me. The man who created my website is a Christian, and He lived in my apartment complex. How ironic is that? As we conversed about the website layout and its purpose, we often discussed God. God sent me a helpmate to ensure that I carried out His mission and my goal. I used the website to blog about my spiritual growth and share the lessons I learned in hopes that they lead others to follow Jesus so they can journey toward living the life that God intends for us to live. The website that was initially created has now been taken down as a new and expanded vision has been set in motion.

I was in financial ruin when God told me to start blogging. I did not have the funds to build a website. God made provisions for me to not only pay the website designer but to continue to build upon it to form it into a business. Yes, God gave me the vision of using my spiritual gift and talent to start a new company.

Yes, we all have a career path that He chose each of us to do so that we can all help build up His kingdom. Shortly after the Holy Spirit filled me, the Lord gave me visions of spiritual gifts that people I knew had. At the time, I did not quite understand why God was giving me this revelation. Now, I fully understand! In 1 Corinthians, Paul tells us about the various spiritual gifts the Holy Spirit gives to each of us. To some, the Spirit gives the gift of healing and to others the gift of prophecy. There are more, but I only named a few to give you an example. In whatever occupation that He chooses to use you, it is all designed to help lead His children to Him. You are to use your spiritual gifts to plant or water seeds. God then will take over and make the seeds grow (see 1 Corinthians 3:5-7).

God wants those who choose to believe in His Son Jesus, as well as those of us who accept the gift of the Holy Spirit, to build His house. God cannot use you to build His kingdom until you accept Jesus, heal from the impurities that have deposited in the dark crevices of your soul, and become humble. Still, some Christians have become lazy and are not operating in their divine purpose, which is why many of you feel unfulfilled and think that God does not hear your prayers. God hears them, and He is continuously coaxing you to move and act. You may ask, "How is he doing it?" One way is by the people He sends to help and encourage you along the way.

If you have not seen the movie "Flight" that stars the actor Denzel Washington, then I invite you to see it. In the movie, you will see a clear demonstration of how God sent people to help lead the main character toward the light, but he kept refusing their help. Some of them wanted to help him out so much that they drifted over to sin to try to save him, which is another trick that the devil uses to tempt you into falling into sin. Jesus is the only one who can save others, not you or me.

As the saying goes, "You can lead a horse to water, but you can't make him drink it." Sometimes you can get so involved with trying to save a family member or friend that you start enabling them to contribute to their bad habits and behavior. Essentially, what you are doing is opening their mouths and pouring the water inside of it, then holding their nose to force them to swallow it because you want to save them. Although your intentions are good, ultimately it creates an even greater problem. Not only does the person you were helping need to be saved, but now you have to get back in line to request repentance because if not you will find yourself in an enormous catastrophic mess.

Take this situation as an example. You have a friend who is addicted to drugs. You see your friend go through withdrawals, and he convinces you that the only way he can live is if he takes drugs. You give in and go with him to purchase the drugs to make sure he is safe. You friend fails to mention that he owes the drug dealer money, so when you two arrive, the dealer demands that you pay for your friend's past due drug payment, with interest. You and the drug dealer get into a dispute, and he shoots you. Now, you are staring death in the face.

Advice to the wise: Watch out for manipulating spirits. When you notice someone depending on you to solve their problems or excessively calling you to get them out of a tight situation, then it is best to resist the temptation to give in, and say "no." It is okay to say no to someone when you know that their requests may set you up to take you away from the will of God. Continue to pray for the person, and let go and allow God to do the rest.

Here is another example: You have just accepted Christ and are trying to live righteously. Then your friend shows up at your front door to invite you to a party. In your heart, you know that you should not attend because of the temptations that will be present at the party. Then your mind begins to play on your heart with thoughts like, "If

I say no, then I may hurt her feelings." "I don't want my friend to think that I feel that I am better than her." You give in and follow your friend to the party where there is drugs and alcohol present. In your past, you were a party-person or club-hopper. Now you have to decide whether to take a drink because you do not want to look different from other people in the crowd. You also do not feel comfortable sharing the Good News with them about Jesus, so you give in to the alcohol and become intoxicated.

The next day you wake up with not only a hangover, but some unknown person is lying in your bed. Then the enemy called "guilt" creeps in and you feel unworthy and fall back into sin that quickly. The devil cannot hurt you. The only thing he can do is play mind games with you so that you go out there and harm yourself or someone else. Tackle the devil of your mind, slam him onto the ground, and walk over him. God has equipped us with the tools, and He grants us grace and mercy to give us countless chances to defeat and conquer our enemies.

Chapter Ten

The Ultimate Command: In Everything You Do, Choose Love

"Let no debt remain outstanding, except the continuing

debt to love one another, for he who loves his

fellowman has fulfilled the law." —Romans 13:8

God is love, and he shows us just how much he loves us in numerous ways. One way that God demonstrates His love for us is through His grace and mercy. God gives us countless chances to get it right and make better choices. He does not give us reprimands for getting it wrong. We reprimand ourselves when we go against God's Word and follow Satan, the ruler of this world. For instance, you know you should not engage in fornication, but so many of you do it anyway. You allowed lust and a temporary pleasure to lead you closer to Satan's pit of burning sulfur. God, however, grants you grace by allowing you to walk away, and He gives you another opportunity to try again. I know God has granted me grace in this same situation just as he has given some of you who are reading this book. However, it is not wise to keep practicing sin because eventually your wrong actions and thoughts will catch up with you.

God's grace is the only reason I am still alive because Lord knows that if it had not been for Jesus, I would have surely perished. I cannot say thank you God enough times for sending your son Jesus to save me. I sacrifice myself daily to be more Christ-like in my thoughts and actions. What I found to be most important is to understand and accept where you are in life and show yourself compassion for trying. We are not perfect, and God loves us in spite of our imperfections. I use to beat myself up whenever I did something that was out of alignment to Jesus character. Sending his son Jesus here to save us is God's ultimate redeeming feature, and only those who accept Him and choose to follow His way will He allow into the kingdom of Heaven.

God created us to love and honor Him, and one another. Our ultimate purpose for being here on earth is to love. You are uniquely designed to serve others with love in whatever capacity you are involved. Although Satan is the ruler of this world, God gave us weapons of mass destruction to kill Satan and defeat our enemies. Love is the one of those weapons that he gave us. If you are operating in love in all that you do, then you are following God's greatest commandment. Love holds the power to defeat your enemies. Satan sends difficult people in your life to cause you to sin against them when you should love them in spite of their transgressions against you. When you are in conflict with someone, it is easy for you to fall victim to Satan's evil ploys.

For instance, my relationship with my dad was plagued with dislike, disdain, and disrespect because we could not resolve our conflicts. The main reason is that we just did not communicate. Communication, when carried out effectively, holds the key to solving many of your conflicts. Some people, however, are not willing to be vulnerable enough to share their emotions or feelings. Therefore, the communication is not open and honest, and the real issue never gets resolved. That is why Jesus has to heal us of so much emotional baggage because we try to keep to our battles a secret.

A majority of the conflicts you have with others are internal, and those internal conflicts trigger an external response called "confrontation." If you hear about people being promiscuous and committing suicide or murders because they try to handle or confront the heavy burdens themselves. Conflict can also cause you to be in confrontation with family members, friends, and even yourself. If you do not handle the confrontation appropriately, you may end up cutting people off or end relationships immaturely without following Jesus' way to resolve the conflict effectively. Jesus gives these instructions to follow when someone sins against you. Matthew 18:15-17 says, "If your brother sins against you, go and show him his fault, just between the two of you. If he listens to you, you have won your brother over. Nevertheless, if he will not listen, take one or two others along, so that every matter may be established by the testimony of two or three witnesses. If he refuses to listen to them, tell it to the church; and if he refuses to listen even to the church, treat him as you would a pagan or tax collector."

When I battled with insecurities, I felt that I was not deserving of having a real and honest man in my life because of my relationship with my dad. The internal battles I dealt with led me to sleep with men who I knew were incapable of loving me the way God intends for a man to love a woman because they were battling their demons. They were no closer to walking with Christ than I was, so we were all falling closer to the depths of Hades. The blind leading the blind— there is truth in that statement.

Love holds the power to destroy all the negative emotions and perceptions brewing inside of you. Regardless of what someone from your past has done to betray you, it is imperative that you love them past their faults. It does not mean that you have to continue having a relationship with them because sometimes wisdom will require you to end the relationship so that you do not get tempted to sin. You can demonstrate love for a person who hurt you by letting go of the pain, releasing the anger and resentment so that you can genuinely pray for the person. Then you can move on with your life, instead of being stuck in a negative mindset about the person or situation.

Hand the situation over to God and learn the lesson that was provided to teach you, and He will do the rest of the work. Keep in mind that when someone wrongs you, especially if that person is not a believer; he will not openly admit his mistakes to you. Instead, he may accuse you or attack your character, all while spitting in your face. Yes, it takes a lot of Godly character to love someone like that, but God commands us to love even our enemies.

When your enemy realizes that he cannot move you by his evil tirades, the demonic presence within him will flee because God is with you. God will take over your battle and win. You must love your enemies to show them that Jesus Christ lives through you, in hopes that they too accept Him into their hearts so they can embrace true love. Charge their transgressions to their head and not their heart for they are acting out of ignorance. Remember where you came from and know that someone had to love you past your transgressions too. Make sure that everything you do and say comes from a loving and clean heart.

When I truly became a follower of Jesus God instructed me to write again. This time, I was obedient, and He released his healing authority into my life. One of the first lessons that I learned during the healing process was to let go of my insecurities and past disappointments through love. I love Jesus too much to toss away all the hard work and sacrifices He made to save me, so slowly I released my selfish pride, arrogance, bitterness and resentment, and I chose to chase after love. I made a decision to love others and myself. I even love those in my life who were the most difficult for me to love. Although I may not have a relationship with them, I can honestly pray for them just as I do for the people whom I can love easily.

Deep down, truthfully speaking, I do not want anyone left out of the Book of Life. I want everyone to enter Heaven with me, even my enemies—the ones who betrayed me. I sincerely want you to let go of your past hurts, heal and live in love like Jesus commands. If you feel like no one loves you or you are unworthy of love, then know that God loves you, Jesus loves you, and I love you too.

The devil is a liar. Do not listen to him because you are worthy of love, peace, joy and happiness. God is love, and if you choose Him, He will be with you every step of the way. He chose you and set you apart from the rest for a divine purpose. You may feel not good enough, not pretty or handsome enough, or smart enough to accomplish something that God is calling you to do. I felt that way about myself too because I was comparing myself to worldly standards. Of course, the ruler of this world does not want to see you progress and grow in the spirit of the Lord. He wants to keep you in a lonely dark corner or place blinders over your eyes to keep you from seeing his evil tactics so that you continue to depend on his worldly system, and drag you right to the pit of Hades along with him. God has a plan for your life, so to Him, you are significant and worthy of praise.

"Brothers, think of what you were when you were called. Not many of you were wise by human standards; not many were influential; not many were noble at birth. But God chose the foolish things of the world to shame the wise; God chose the weak things of the world to shame the strong. He chose the lowly things of this world and the despised things and the things that are not to nullify the things that are so that no one can boast before him (1 Corinthians 1:26-28)."

If God gives you His stamp of approval, then there is nothing that can hold you back from living your dreams and honoring Him. "Therefore, as it is written: Let him who boasts boast in the Lord (1Corithinians 1:31)."

Chapter Eleven

The Certification: Your Changed Life Certifies You to Share the Good News

"How beautiful on the mountains are the feet of those who bring good news." —Isaiah 52:7

Before I answered the call on my life, I existed but was not alive. I felt empty and unfulfilled with my life. I thought that a man, beauty, house and a career would validate me. I began to chase after those superficial and materialistic items thinking that it would make me feel complete. It did make me feel whole for a season, but just like when a new car scent wears off so did my false sense of happiness and contentment. I was battling with temptation and sin that kept me in the dark shadow of death. The further I followed the world, the deeper I sank into its thick and immovable quicksand, called the middle ground. I became inflexible and set in my ways, so it is not surprising that rheumatoid arthritis set in my joints.

I remember a quote that I implemented in my life, which is, "It's my way or the highway." I wanted things to go my way, and when disappointment came, I did not handle it well, at all. If something went wrong or I had a dispute with someone, externally I would place the blame on the other person. However, internally I was throwing heavy weights of negative thoughts in my mind that consistently weighed me down throughout my early adult life. The tape recorder in my mind would switch to play when I faced a challenge or disappointment, and I would hear comments such as these, "She is better than you, that is why he is with her and not you." "You are a failure." "Your daddy does not want you either; that is why he left."

The negative messages playing in my mind played a part in how I handled stress, disappointments. I beat myself up to the point that I became sick with a disease that has caused my autoimmune system to attack my healthy joint cells. I was mentally tearing myself down, and then my body turned against me and began to beat me up, too. Thank God for sending Jesus here to heal me from the emotional baggage that the ruler of this world used to try to kill me. Jesus restored me to an even better person than I was before. I feel brand new and free from the worldly system.

During the healing process, the Holy Spirit instructed me to learn the descendants of Jesus, so I studied Jesus' family lineage.

Then Jesus took my hand and we journeyed down my family line to a point when I was a little girl. He showed me how Satan deceived the old me. I say the "old me" because I am a completely different person than I was before. Satan placed these thoughts in my mind when I was too young and not strong enough in the Word of God to resist them. The door opened for Satan to enter my mind when my dad and mom were not getting along and fighting, and that is how he gets inside our mind most of the time.

When I accepted Christ as a young girl, Satan deceived me again by telling me to stop loving my dad and to cut him out of my life. Then after I gave in to him, he sent his troops to keep me under attack and in the dark. Every time he saw me getting closer to God, he would send a distraction my way. In my case, the distraction was usually a man. When a man came in my life, I would lose my Godly sense and give in because I did not want to be alone. That was Satan's way of fooling me because I would fall victim to believing in a man's love over God's love. I was chasing the man for love when I should have been chasing after Jesus.

I never felt good about giving my body and temple to a man who I was not married or in a loving, committed relationship. I struggled with it because in my heart I knew it was wrong. There are scriptures in the Bible that tell us that we should not fornicate, but many of us do it anyway. I also struggled with honoring men who did not follow Jesus and implement His teachings in their life. I am not saying he had to be perfect, but his character should show that he has a genuine heart for God. If his actions showed me that he could not love me with mutual respect, compassion, and integrity then eventually I would walk away from the relationship. I felt turmoil inside when a man would do or say things to me to get me to have sex with him when I knew in my heart that the only man I should allow entering my temple is the man who honors and respect God. In the Old Testament God refers to the children of Israel as adulterers because they did not keep their commitment to Him. We are like the children of Israel too. God comes and delivers us from evil or dangerous situations, and we vow to follow him. Then shortly after He bails us out of the situation, we go back to our old ways and habits, forgetting the countless miracles God performed in our lives.

When I made a decision to accept Jesus and follow his ways God gave me a white stone with a new name on it. Since I, with the Lord's help, overcame my enemies and defeated them God gave me some of the hidden manna. He opened my eyes and began showing me how the Babylonian system—the world—operates. He also began stripping away the old ways I lived, and now he teaches me His way to live. He had me get rid of the secular music I listened to because it led me to have negative thoughts. Now, I listen to music that uplifts my mood and produces positive thoughts and emotions.

I do not watch television as much because I became sensitive to the images of the money-oriented and artificial "reality shows" that are on most of the stations. I clearly see how the world sets up people who lack the spiritual understanding to fall deeper into sin and remain committed to following Satan's way of life, which is full of deceit and disillusion.

Now, when I go to church, the pastor confirms or clarifies the things that God has already taught me. God sent people in my life to plant his seed in me when I was a little girl. I battled with accepting the truth because of the false worldly messages and so-called "realities" that Satan used against me that contradicted what I knew in my heart was true. My family, friends as well as my church family, planted and watered the seed, but God grew it (see 1 Corinthians 3:6).

I can tell you this, and I know this is true. The truth is not how it appears in the physical realm because Satan has manipulated this world into following false pretenses. It takes bravery and courage to follow the truth and go against the grain so that you can defeat Satan and his massive army of false perceptions that appear to be real. You must link up with Jesus to receive all of the promises that God gives to his children.

Let me share with you what God showed me through His son Jesus. Jesus sent me the promise of the Holy Spirit. The Holy Spirit guides and instructs my daily activities. By listening to the Holy Spirit, I can discern whether to turn right, stop or turn left. Jesus teaches me how to live the way God wants us to live. Satan, the ruler of this world, sets up the things of this world to appear as though they were real. The false reality that he sets up is not your reality unless you believe it. Satan does not try new tricks. He typically uses the same devices every time. Here is an example of how your reality could be a setup, and if you are not following the Holy Spirit, you will be misled and fall into repeated patterns of sin.

For instance, Satan has some women thinking that they have to look a certain way or have the body structure of a curvy dancer to get a man or husband. This thought can lead women to develop insecurities about their physical appearance, which makes them feel unwanted, unloved, and unappreciated. Those insecurities cause many women to give in to the temptation of having sex with men prematurely—before marriage or life commitment. Your body is God's temple so every time you fornicate you commit sin against your body. In the Bible, it states to flee from sexual sins because it defiles your body. All other sins do not affect your body (see 1 Corinthians 6:18-20).

Let me take it a step further. The music that he has some of our most talented artists produce, sing, and rap, is set up to entice you to sin when you repeat the filthy lyrics. While listening to the song, you find yourself not only singing the song but also thinking about it. Lastly, it leads you to follow through with acting it out, either with your body or some other form of evil action.

This so-called recession or famine that the world is facing is yet another way to keep people in a place of need and trapped in its system. Therefore, you consistently lack more of the necessities that you need to survive causing added stress and tension in the home. Satan brings financial stress into your home, and that pressure drives the knife-carver named "division" to use his tools to cut and destroy families. Statistics tell us that in the United States forty to fifty percent of married couples divorce. Wow! The statistics for divorce are even greater for people in their second or third marriage. It starts out when the couple's trust gets shattered. They begin to accuse one another of misdeeds and, if they have children, it opens the door for Satan to set his trap for them, too.

Every day I work toward being more Christ-like by replacing my old lifestyle with the new way of life through Jesus Christ. His Holy Spirit leads me to certain scriptures in the Bible, delivers the Word of God, and teaches me how to live righteously. God has called me to teach you the things that he has shared with me so that you can heal from your past, live in the present, and prepare for your future life with Him in His Kingdom. God loves you so much that He came to earth to help us. He chooses those who are witnesses of Jesus to share the Good News and to teach others about Him so that His light can shine through us.

If you are reading this and you feel a tug in your heart prompting you to come and accept His hand, do not delay any longer. God wants to heal you just as he healed me. He has so much in store for you. He wants you to experience a love that goes beyond what words can express. He wants to give you peace of mind so that you can build and prosper in every area of your life. God does not want you fooled by Satan any longer. He has all the tools you will need to defeat Satan and his troops. Remember that in your weakness; you are strong through Christ.

Christ died so that we can live. His spirit lives in each of us who accept Him. It is funny how the different religions believe in God, follow biblical principles, yet refuse to accept Jesus. Are you going to continue to follow the traditions of man and allow Satan to deceive you, or will you take Jesus' hand and enjoy the fruit of the spirit? God allowed me to experience the trials and test that I eventually overcame so that He could refine and build my character to prepare me for His work, and to become a valuable member of His family. I am a child of God, and He is my Father and those that He calls, serve Him. I told my story to honor and glorify my Lord. It was written to lead you to Jesus because I love you too much to leave you behind.

As I mentioned earlier, God gave each of us a unique gift, and He wants us to use it to perform a career, job or start a business that is designed specifically for you. When you are operating in your gift or talent, it will honor and glorify Him as well as prepare you, as well as others, for His kingdom. He has called you to help build His kingdom. If you have slipped back into following the world or you just do not believe in the Son of God, then this is your test. Psalm 66:9-12 reads, "He has preserved our lives and kept our feet from slipping. For you, O God tested us; you refined us like silver. You brought us into prison and laid burdens on our backs. You let men rid over our heads; we went through the fire and water, but you brought us to a place of abundance."

Are you ready to pass the test by rededicating your life to Christ or accepting that Jesus died on the cross to save you? If you believe in your heart and are ready to accept and follow Him, then repeat this prayer. Lord, you of all others know that I have sinned and fallen short of the Glory of God. Thankfully, you sent your holy son Jesus to suffer the punishment that I so deserve. Jesus loves me so much that he died and rose from the dead to save me so that I may have eternal life. I humbly accept Him into my heart and life from this day and forever. Amen! Here is the Bible's base evidence of this fact. "God so loved the world that he gave his one and only Son so that whoever believes in him may not be lost, but have eternal life."

(John 3:10.) Jesus is the only One, who can save people. No one else in the world is able to save us" (Acts 4:12).

I am about to share a secret with you. Now that you have accepted Christ into your heart, all you must do is just believe in His word, accept and follow His gift of the Holy Spirit and in everything that you do, do it with love in your heart. Where there is love God is there with you, and no guilt, shame or condemnation will fall upon you. Jesus died to wipe away all of your sins. Therefore, you will not fall under the curse of the law unless you decide not to accept the truth. God's protective grace will cover you every step of your journey. I encourage you to connect with a spirit-filled community, read positive, encouraging, and motivating books, blogs, or scriptures daily, and follow Christ all of the way to your glory. If you need help on this journey, all you have to do is ask for it. God will send you the answers as well as put His angels in position so that you will not strike your foot on a stone.

You have already taken the most important step by accepting Jesus into your heart. Keep this in mind as you walk with Christ, that anything is possible through Him who strengthens you (see Philippians 4:13). I am so happy and excited for you. I cannot wait to see you grow and accomplish great things in this lifetime and beyond.

Notes

Scripture references and quotations are from the Holy Bible, the New International Version. Copyright © 2002 by the Zondervan Corporation.

About the Author

Na'Toria serves as a personal development coach, writer, consultant, and inspirational speaker. Na'Toria has the gift of counseling and guidance. She has the innate ability to see the world from the perspective of others as she guides and coaches them toward living the lifestyle that they want and deserve. Her business follows the spiritual principle to serve others with love to help restore harmony and peace in the life of those that she coaches.

Na'Toria obtained her master's degree in counseling education and a bachelor's degree in elementary education. She is also a certified school counselor and teacher. She has a passion for helping children who are emotionally hurt, develop coping skills so that their heart and mind can heal and they can excel academically. Na'Toria also enjoys teaching children character development so that they can become a principled contributing member of society.

Na'Toria resides in Florida with her two children. In her spare time, she enjoys reading, journaling, listening to music, dancing, watching movies and hanging out with her family and friends.

Printed in the United States
By Bookmasters